MANAGEMENT
THOUGHTS AND FUNCTIONS

By

Dr. M. Karthikeyan
Associate Professor
Department of Cooperatives
Institute of Cooperatives & Development Studies
Ambo University
Ambo, Ethiopia
Email: mkeya2003@gmail.com

&

Dr. Assefa Gebre
Associate Professor
College of Agriculture
Adama University
Ethiopia
Email: assefagebre2003@gmail.com

DISCOVERY PUBLISHING HOUSE PVT. LTD.
NEW DELHI-110 002

Published by:
Tilak Wasan
DISCOVERY PUBLISHING HOUSE PVT. LTD.
4383/4B, Ansari Road, Darya Ganj
New Delhi-110 002 (India)
Phone : +91-11-23279245; 23253475; 43596065
E-mail : discoverybooksindia@gmail.com
discoverypublishinghouse@gmail.com
namitwasan9@gmail.com
web : www.discoverypublishinggroup.com

***First Edition:* 2018**

ISBN: 978-93-5056-443-1

Management (*Thoughts and Functions*)

Printed at:
Infinity Imaging Systems
Delhi

Preface

Dear Readers! It is our pleasure to introduce the book on "**Management *(Thoughts & Functions)***" to you. It has been designed in a detailed manner so as to help you understand the basic concepts of management and managerial functions. This book dovetails the management theories and thoughts, and managerial functions: planning, organizing, staffing, directing and controlling.

This work is based on our experience as teacher, trainer and researcher in the field of management for more than 16 years. The present work is the outcome of our experience and many articles published in reputed journals. This book will be very much useful to the students, researchers, trainers in various management training establishments and managers of different firms. We have drawn the inputs from various materials; papers, journals, books and we have consulted several of our friends, colleagues and field experts. We are ever grateful and thankful to them for their immense support and healthy criticism. We hope that the readers of this book will get knowledge on management. Any useful comments, suggestions to improve the present version are welcome and solicited from the readers. We are thankful to Discovery Publishing House Pvt. Ltd., New Delhi, for publishing this book neatly under its renowned label for the management knowledge community.

M.Karthikeyan

Assefa Gebre

Contents

Management
An Overview

MEANING AND DEFINITION

Considerable attention has been drawn to the need for effective management in both public and private sector organisations. In most developing countries, the concern for effective management has been the result of fear of failure and disillusionment about competence in the public sector and acute competition in the private sector. Even in developed market economies, the concern for effective management has continued to be a way of not only maintaining the leadership status of organisations and their members but logical means of improving the quality of the goods and services to the population.

What is Management?

The term management can have different meanings and it is important that we understand these different definitions.

Management is *a process* involving certain functions and activities that managers must perform. Managers also use principles in managing which are generally accepted tenets that guide their thinking and actions. This is what managers do. They engage in the process of management. *Management Principles and Functions* focus on this management process, the functions managers perform, and the principles they apply in managing organisations.

Management may be defined as the process of planning, organising, leading, staffing and controlling the controlling of organisation members and using all other organisational resources to achieve set goals. A process is a systematic way of doing things and management is a process because all managers regardless of their particular aptitudes or skills, engage in certain interrelated activities in order to achieve their desired goals. Since the late nineteenth century, it has been common practice to define management in terms of usually four functions of managers: planning, organising, leading, and controlling.

Robert Presthus, 1962 defined management as the process by which individuals and group efforts is coordinated towards group gaols. J.H Donnelly and others (1977) have given the same definition to management as "management is the process by which individuals and group efforts is coordinated towards group gaols"

Koontz and Weibrich/1990/defined management as "Management is the process of designing and maintaining an environment in which individuals working together in groups, efficiently and effectively to accomplish selected aims." This basic definition contains the following points.

1. Managers carry out the managerial function of planning, organising, staffing, leading and controlling.
2. Management is applicable to any form of organisation/ profit oriented organisations and non-profit oriented organisations.
3. Management applies to managers at all organisational levels.
4. The aim of all managers the same – to maximise benefits.
5. Managing is concerned with productivity: this implies efficiency and effectiveness.

The system–type definition viewed by Louis E Boone and David L Kurtz (1984) has been "Management is the use of people and other resources to accomplish objectives".

Some management writers have defined "Management as the process of planning, organising, leading and controlling the efforts of organisation members and using all other organisational resources to achieve started organisational goals."

J.L. Lundy (1992) has given the following definition of management, which is as "management is principally a task of planning, coordinating, motivating and controlling the efforts of others towards the specific objectives.

Henri Fayol, the father of modem management, defines management as "To forecast and plan, to organise to command, to coordinate and to control" the functions of organisations in order to achieve the organisation objectives.

The American Association says that: "management is a function of guiding human and physical resources into dynamic organisation units which attain their objectives". "W. Jack Duncan (1975) describes, "Management consists of all organisational activities that involve goal formation and accomplishment, performance appraisal, and the development of an operating philosophy that ensures the organisation's survival with the social system."

Harold Koontz and Cyril O'Donnell (1972) have defined management as that "management creates and maintains internal environment in an enterprise. Where individuals working together in groups, and performs efficiently and effectively towards the attainment of group goals. It is an art of getting the work done through and with people in formally organised groups".

SIGNIFICANCE AND NATURE OF MANAGEMENT

1. Management is basically multidisciplinary. It draws knowledge and concepts from various disciplines such as psychology, sociology, anthropology, economics ecology, statistics, operation research, history etc.
2. Management principles are relative, not absolute, and they should be applied according to the need of organisation.

3. Management is a science, or art. There is a controversy whether it is a science or art. However, management, is both a science and an art.
4. Management has been regarded as a profession by many while many have suggested that it has not achieved that status.
5. Management is a universal phenomenon. However, management principles are not universally applicable but are to be modified according to the needs of the situation.
6. Management principles are dynamic and flexible and change with the changes in the environment in which organisation exists.

The Process of Management

The process of management consists of certain basic *management functions.* The management process is an integrated whole. However, something as complex as the management process is more easily understood when it is described as a series of separate activities or functions making up the entire process. The management functions are *planning, organising, staffing and controlling,* linked together by *leading.* Planning determines what results the organisation will achieve; organising specifies *how* it will achieve the results; and controlling determines *whether* the results are achieved. Throughout planning, organising, and controlling, managers exercise leadership.

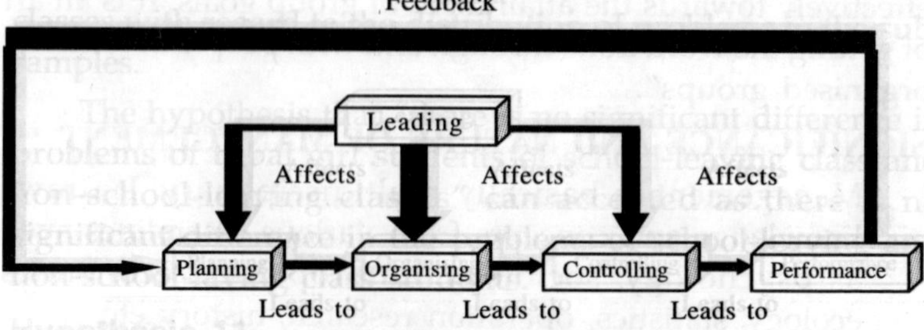

***Fig. 1.1:* The Management Process**

Source: Ivancevich, Donnelly and Gibson, Management: Principles and Functions; 4th Edition, Boston, 1989, p. 6 USA.

LEVELS AND TYPES OF MANAGEMENT

As any organisation increases in size and complexity, its management must adapt by becoming more specialised. Some results of specialisation of the management process are discussed as follows.

Type of Managers

The history of most ongoing firms reveals an evolution through which the management has grown from one manager with many subordinates to a team of many managers with many subordinates. The development of different types of managers has occurred as a result of this evolution (Figures 1.2, 1.3, 1.4, and 1.5).

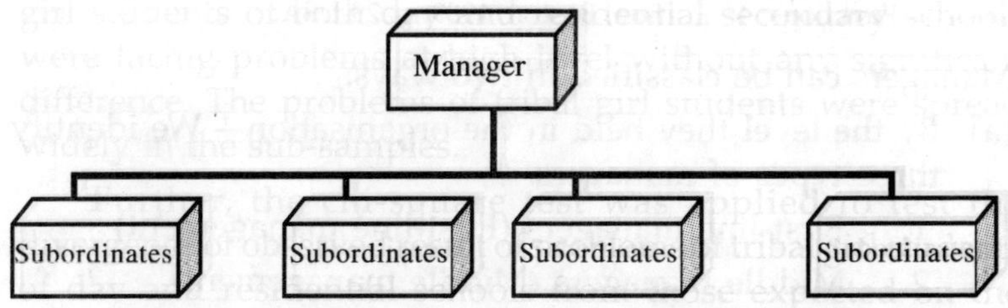

Fig. 1.2: **One Manager and many Subordinates**

Source: Ivancevich, Donnelly and Gibson, Management: Principles and Functions; 4th Edition, Boston, 1989, p. 28 USA.

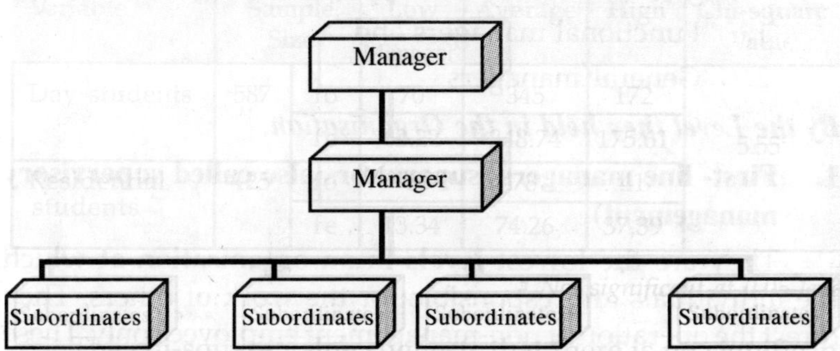

Fig. 1.3: **Vertical Specialisation of the Management Process**

Source: Ivancevich, Donnelly and Gibson, Management: Principles and Functions; 4th Edition, Boston, 1989, p. 28 USA.

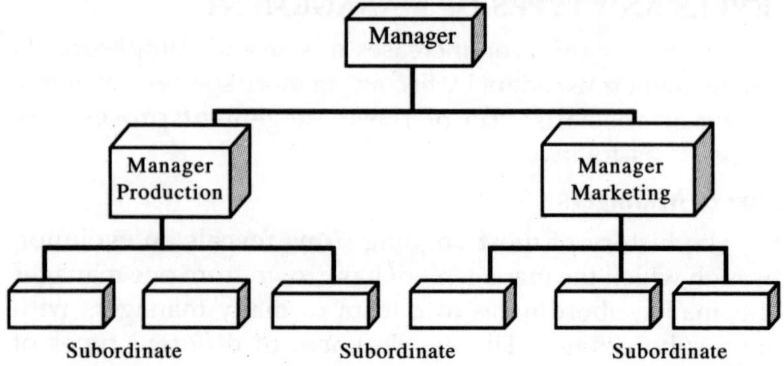

***Fig.1.4:* Horizontal Organisation of the Management Process**

Source: Ivancevich, Donnelly and Gibson, Management: Principles and Functions; 4th Edition, Boston, 1989, p. 29 USA.

Managers can be classified in two ways:

(a) By the level they held in the organisation – We identify three types of managers.
   1. First-line managers (First-line management)
   2. Middle managers (Middle management)
   3. Top level managers (Top management)

(b) By the range of organisational activities for which they are responsible (by the scope of activities managers manage)- We identify two types of managers
   1. Functional managers and
   2. General managers

By the Level they held in the Organisation

1. First- line managers (supervisors also called supervisory management)

They are the lowest levels in an organisation at which the individuals are responsible for the work of others. They direct the operation of non-management employees only. These managers coordinate the work of others who are not managers themselves. Managers at the level of first-line management are often called supervisors, office managers, or foremen.

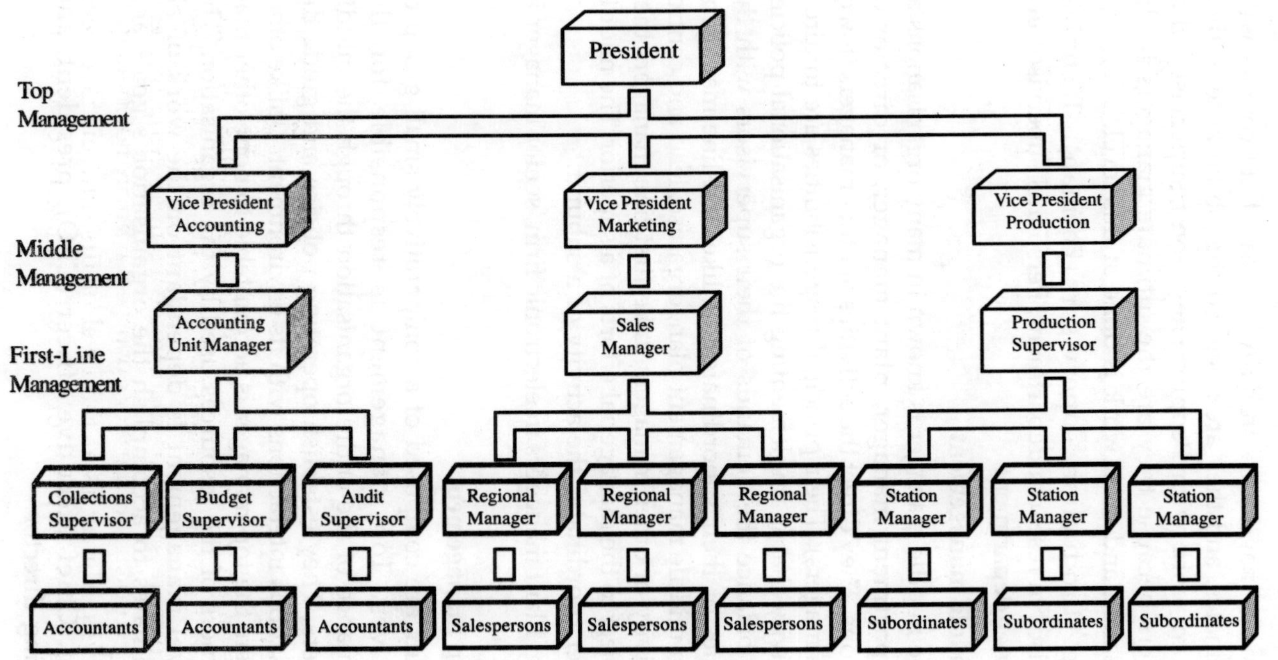

Fig. 1.5: Vertical and Horizontal Specialisation of the Management Process

Source: Ivancevich, Donnelly and Gibson, Management: Principles and Functions; 4th Edition, Boston, 1989, p. 30 USA

First-line managers are in daily or near daily contact with subordinates, and they are assigned the job because of their ability to work with People. They don't supervise other managers because they are the ultimate managers in the organisation and most work is done at this level.

E.g. Production supervisor (Forman), Technical supervisor in research department, Personnel supervisor in a personnel department

2. Middle management

The middle manager is known in many organisations as the department manager, plant manager, or director of operations. They direct the activities of other managers (lower level managers). Their principal responsibilities are to direct the activity that is implementing the organisational policies and to balance the demands of their supervisors with the capacities of their subordinates. Unlike first-line managers, those in middle management plan, organise, lead and control the activity of other managers. Like first-line managers they are subject to the managerial efforts of a superior. The middle manager coordinates the activity of a subunit.

E.g. Plant managers in electronic firm, senior manager in a bank.

3. Top management

They are composed of a comparatively small group of executives. Top management is responsible for the performance of the entire organisation through the middle managers. They establish operating policies and guide the organisations interactions with its environment. Unlike other managers the top manager is accountable to none other than the owners of the resources used by the organisation. The top-level management is dependant on the work of all subordinates to accomplish the organisation's goals and mission.

E.g. Chief executive officer (CEO), president, and managing director

Based on scope of activities managers can be classified as:

1. Functional managers
2. General manager

Organisations are often described as a set of functions. A function in this sense is a collection of similar activities. For example the marketing function consists of sales, promotion, distribution and market research activities.

1. Functional managers

As the management process becomes horizontally specialised, a functional manager is responsible for only one functional area (for only one organisational activity) such as production, accounting or marketing.

2. General Manager

This oversees a complex unit such as a company, subsidiary or an independent operative division. He/she is responsible for all the activities of the units such as production, marketing and others. It is important to remember that functional and general managers alike pian, organise, lead and control relationships over time. The difference is in the scope of activities that they oversee.

MANAGEMENT: AN ART? A SCIENCE?

The question of whether management is an art or a science or both is a common one in the discipline's literature. A basic understanding of this issue is crucial to the discussion of management that follows.

Science is a systematic study that leads to a general body of knowledge about a subject. The historical framework of management clearly indicates that management has been the target of systematic study for centuries and those general principles or concepts have been derived from this effort. Most observers would classify management as a developing science.

Before answering to the question whether management is an art or a science, it is good to understand what artistic management and scientific management are.

Scientific Management

Scientific management can be defined as the use of codified and verified knowledge in the planned management of any organised activity. Scientific management often involves such tools as motion-and-time studies (studies to determine whether a particular act can be performed more quickly and efficiently) and research to ensure that personnel are being used effectively. Scientific management tends to be analytical, statistical, rational and quantifiable.

Artistic Management

Management is also an art. In fact, one source has even defined-management as the "art of making decisions with insufficient information." The artistic process is generally seen as having three vital aspects: *craft, vision, and communication*. The process of management qualifies as an art form in all instances managers must have the tools (craft) to accomplish their tasks. They must possess order to implement innovative strategies, and they must be able to communicate effectively in the work environment and elsewhere. Artistic management, in contrast, can be defined as the conscientious use of skill and creative imagination in planning and executing the goals of the organisation. Artistic management tends to be subjective, no statistical, emotional, common-sensical and behavioural.

A balanced perspective suggests that management is both an art and a science. The management process follows the general scenario for the artistic process. But its craft or tool aspects are clearly based on a scientific body of knowledge that has been accumulated over time.

Remember that both scientific and artistic elements are involved in the management process. Progressive management uses scientific management when possible. But in those situations in which scientific measurement cannot be used, managers resort to the artistic approach.

THE UNIVERSALITY OF MANAGEMENT FUNCTIONS

Regardless of the title, position or management level, all managers do the same job. All managers execute the five management functions (function of planning, organising, staffing, leading, and controlling) and work through and with others and achieve organisational objectives. Figure 1.6 shows the concept known as universality of management. Although all managers perform the same function, the various management levels require different amount of time for each function, and the points of emphasis in each function will differ. For example, first-line managers usually spend less time planning than do top managers. However they spend much more time and effort leading and controlling. At high levels in the organisation, far more time is spent planning and less time is spent leading. The amount of time and effort devoted to organising, staffing and controlling are usually fairly equal at all levels of management. Please notice that in figure 1-6 the staffing function is considered, as part of the organising function of management and therefore the time required for the levels of management is more or less similar to that of organising function.

Top management: Top-level management's job is concerned with the big picture of the organisation. The planning function for top-level management consists of developing the major purpose of organisation, the global objectives for organisational accomplishment, and the major policy statements for implementation by middle and first-line managers. Organising at this level is viewed as developing the overall structure of the organisation to support the accomplishment of the plans and then acquiring the resources for the firm. The staffing function at the top-level of management is concerned with policy development in the areas of equal opportunity in employment and with employee development. Top management is also concerned with acquiring talent to fill upper–management positions. The emphasis is directing on organisation wide management philosophy on cultivating an organisational climate for optimal employee performance. The controlling function at this level emphasizes the overall organisation performance relative to organisation objectives.

Middle management: Middle-level management's primary job is to develop implementation strategies for the broad concepts determined by top-level management. For example, if the top-level managers decide 10 per cent of profit objective, the job of the middle managers is to translate that goal into concrete goal of their own so that the desired profit can be attained. Middle managers decide on how to do it, with new products, new customers, and new territories. Organising at the middle-level means making specific adjustments in the organisation structure and allocating resources acquired by top management. Staffing focuses on the policy implementation in the areas of equal employment opportunity and employee development programmes. Directing is viewed as providing leadership and support for lower level management. Controlling is concerned with monitoring the results of plans for specific products, regions, and subunits and making the indicated adjustment to achieve organisational objectives.

First-line management: Whereas top-level management is concerned with the big picture and middle-level management with organisation wide implementation, first-line management is concerned with only its immediate responsibilities. For the first-line manager, planning involves scheduling employees, deciding what work will be done first and developing procedures to achieve the goals. Organising must consist of delegating authority or deciding that work done by one group of people should be done by another work group. Staffing at this level consists of requesting a new employee, hiring that employee, and then training the person to perform the job. Directing includes communicating and providing leadership both to the work group and employees individually. Controlling at this level focuses on having thee manager's work group meet its production, sales or quality, objectives.

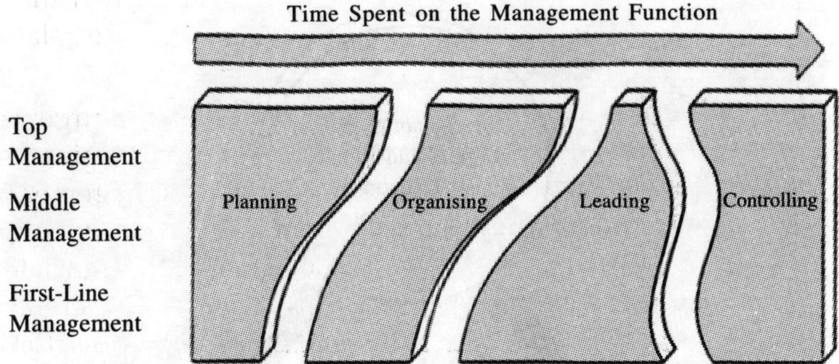

Fig. 1.6: **Management Levels and Management Functions**

Source: Ivancevich, Donnelly and Gibson, Management: Principles and Functions; 4th Edition, Boston, 1989, p. 31 USA.

MANAGERIAL ROLES

Henry Mintzberg combined his own study with existing research in all kinds and levels of managers. He said that there is considerable similarity in the behaviour of managers at all levels.

All managers, he argued, have formal authority over their own organisational units and derive status from that authority. The status causes all managers to be involved in interpersonal relations with subordinates, peers, and supervisors who in turn provide managers with the information they need to make decisions. He determined managers in ten (10) different but closely related managerial roles the ten roles can be separated into three categories: interpersonal roles, informational roles and decisional roles. See figure 1.7.

1. Interpersonal roles

The three roles of figurehead, leader and liaison grow out of the manager's formal authority and focus on interpersonal relationships. This helps the manager to keep the organisation going smoothly. Thus, although the duties associated with these roles are often routine, manager can't ignore them.

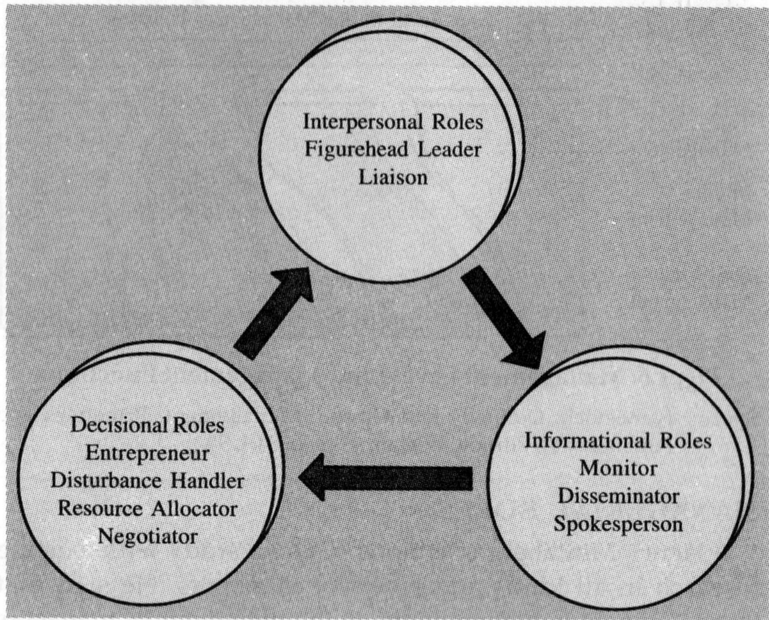

Fig. 1.7: **Managerial Roles**

Source: Ivancevich, Donnelly and Gibson, Management: Principles and Functions; 4th Edition, Boston, 1989, p. 37 USA.

Figurehead Role

All managerial jobs require some duties that are symbolic and ceremonial in nature. As a head of a department or a unit, the manager acts as a figurehead by performing certain ceremonial duties like a college dean who hands out diplomas at graduation, greeting visitors, attending a subordinate's weeding, taking a customer to lunch etc.

Leadership Role

The manager's role involves directing and coordinating the activities of subordinates. This involves staffing (hiring, training, promoting and dismissing) and motivating employees. The leadership role also involves controlling to make sure that things are going according to plan. First line managers, in particular, feel that effectiveness in this role is essential for successful job performance.

Liaison Role

The liaison role involves managers in interpersonal roles outside of their area of command. This role may involve contacts both inside and outside the organisation. The managers' play the liaison role by dealing with people other than subordinates or superiors such as peers with in the organisation and suppliers or clients from outside the organisation.

2. Informational Role

Managers need information in order to make the right decisions and others people in the managers unit or organisation depend on the information they receive from and transmit through manager. The *informational role* establishes the manager as the central point for receiving and sending nonroutine information. There are three informational roles in which the manager gathers and disseminates information. They include:

The Monitor Role

The monitor role involves examining the environment in order to gather information, changes, opportunities and problems that may affect the unit. It involves looking for information that can be used to advantage. Subordinates are questioned and unsolicited information is also collected, usually through the managers system of personal contacts. The manager is supposed to be the best-informed member of his group. The formal and informal contacts developed in the liaison role are often useful here.

The Disseminator Role

This involves the distribution of important or privileged information to subordinates.

The Spokesperson Role

In the spokesperson role, the manager represents. This representation may be internal when a manager makes the case for salary increases to top management. It may also be external when an executive represents the organisation's view on a particular issue of public interest to a local civic organisation. One of the important roles of spokesperson is to keep employees in the organisation satisfied by keeping them well-informed about what is going on in and out side the organisation. E.g. when a CEO makes a speech to a group of consumers/clients in behalf of his/her company

3. Decisional Roles

Developing interpersonal relationships and gathering information are important, but they are not ends in themselves. They serve as the basic inputs to the process of decision-making. Managers make decision-using information gathered from various sources. It is believed that decisional roles played by managers include such roles as entrepreneur, disturbance handler, resource allocator, and negotiator.

Role of Entrepreneur

The purpose of the *entrepreneur role* is to change the unit for the better. The effective first-line supervisor is continually looking for new ideas or new methods to improve the unit's performance. The manager tries to improve his work unit. He might come across with a good idea, and he can launch a project helpful to the company.

Role of Disturbance Handler

In the *disturbance handler role,* managers make decisions or take corrective action in response to pressure that is beyond their control. Usually the decisions must be made quickly, which means that this role takes priority over other roles. The immediate goal is to bring about stability. The manager's responds to situations that are beyond his control, such as strike, bankrupt customer, or breach of contract.

Role of Resource Allocator

The resource allocator role places a manager in the position of deciding who will get what resources. These resources include money, people, time, and equipment. Invariably there are not enough resources to go around, and the manager must allocate the scarce goods in many directions. Resource allocation, therefore, is one of the most critical of the manager's decisional roles. A college dean must decide which courses to offer next semester, based on available faculty. The parliament of Ethiopia must decide whether to allocate more to defence and less to social programmes.

Role of Negotiator

In the *negotiator role,* a manager must bargain with other units and individuals to obtain advantages for her unit. The negotiations may concern work, performance, objectives, resources, or anything else influencing the unit. Working out a deal with a consulting firm or a production manager who draws up a contract with supplier. A top-level manager may negotiate with a labour union representative.

Managerial Level and Roles

The level in the organisation will influence which managerial roles are emphasised, although at every level, each role must be performed to some degree. Obviously, top managers spend much more time in the figurehead role than do first-line supervisors. The liaison role of top and middle managers will involve individuals and groups outside the organisation, while at the first-line level; the liaison will be outside the unit but inside the organisation. Top managers must monitor the environment for changes that can influence the entire organisation. Middle managers monitor the environment for changes likely to influence the particular function (for example, marketing) that they manage, and the first-line supervisor is concerned about what will influence his unit.

2 Development of Management Theory

PIONEERING EFFORTS IN MANAGEMENT

Management as a function is as old as civilisation. Management became necessary as soon as human groups and organisations evolved way back into the pre-historic times.

Even the ancient human being who was living in the caves had an organised way of hunting, farming and fishing to supply the whole family with the necessary food items and other materials. Moreover one can also think of how complex the management style of the Egyptian could be to construct their pyramids in a manner that reflect their level of civilization at that time. The skilful and well-planned exodus of Hebrews from Egypt was a monumental management achievement. Records also indicate that the ancient Chinese civilisation also had knowledge management functions.

Although little is written about management during the medieval period, management practices played an extremely important in two influential organisations: the Roman Catholic Church and the military. The Roman Catholic Church is one of the oldest and best-run institutions in history and military organisations with authority relationships have served as a model for many enterprises.

The industrial revolution beginning in the late 18th century changed the entire behavior of the civilised world and gave birth to accelerated rate of resource accumulation and growth of large-scale enterprises. The industrial revolution created its own management problems for the entrepreneur at that time. Managers emphasised to make their own companies as large as possible. They focused mainly on rapidly accumulating workers, machinery, and capital in what amounted to a race to make their companies larger than twice of their competitors. As industries became larger and more complex to organise and run the managers focus started to shift from growth to efficiency.

Constituently, they began to seek new ways of utilising the resources they have accumulated. Increasingly they sought new techniques that would enable them to reduce costs and increase efficiency. It was out of this industrial environment that different concepts and techniques on how to manage business enterprises emerged.

There are different theories of management namely: Scientific management, Administrative management theory, Human relation movement, Behavioral science school, Quantitative management school, System approach, Contingency Theory and so much more. Knowledge about management comes from the field of management itself, individual who practiced management, as well as many other fields. Many individuals whose interest in management was or is strictly scientific have contributed knowledge to the field. Many psychologists, sociologists, and anthropologists consider management to be a very important social phenomenon and managers to be an important social resource. Their interest is strictly scientific; they want to understand and to explain the process of management. Numerous other professions such as mathematics, accounting, economics, law, political science, engineering, and philosophy also have contributed to the discipline of management.

How can we approach the study of the discipline of management in some coherent way? It requires organisation of the knowledge so that it is meaningful to the student of management.

Contemporary management knowledge is the product of three basic approaches:

1. The classical approach;
2. The behavioural approach; and
3. The management science approach.

Through these three approaches, one can see an evolution of what *is* known and what *should be* known about management. Let us examine each one.

CLASSICAL APPROACH

Serious attention to management began in the early years of this century. One of the critical problems facing managers at that time was how to increase the efficiency and productivity of the work force. The classical approach to management can be better understood by examining it from two perspectives. These two perspectives are based on the problems each examined. One perspective concentrated on the problems of lower-level managers dealing with the everyday problems of the work force. This perspective is known as *scientific management.* The other perspective concentrated on the problems of top-level managers dealing with the everyday problems of managing the entire organisation. This perspective is known as *classical organisation theory.*

Scientific Management

Scientific management that introduced scientific methods of management is an important aspect of the classical school of management thought. At the turn of the 20th century, business was expanding and creating new products and new markets, but labour was in short supply.

Two solutions were available:

1. Substitute capital for labour or
2. Use labour more efficiently.

Scientific management concentrated on the second solution.

Fredrick Winslow Taylor: Although Henry Towne is known to have initiated the search for a science of management, the birth of scientific management is often credited to Taylor who is popularly called the father of scientific management.

His published work, "The principles of scientific management", 1911 became the basis of scientific approach to management. He's interested in developing the most scientific (the best way of doing tasks) and rational principles of handling people, machines, materials and money to secure maximum benefit for the employers as well as the employees.

Taylor's philosophy of management rested on four basic principles:

1. *The development of a true science of management,* so that, for example the best method for performing each task could be determined. He felt that for every task there is one best way to do it.
2. *The Scientific selection of workmen:* that is scientifically selecting the best person for the job, training her/him thoroughly in the tasks and procedures to be followed, and giving her/him jobs.
3. *The scientific education and development of workmen:* training employees for best performance.
4. *Intimate* friendly co-operation between management (the planners) and labor (the doers) to ensure that the work is being done according to the established principles and procedures (principles).

In Taylor's other major published works "A piece rate system" (1895), "Shop management" (lower level management) (1903), and "On the art of cutting metals" (1906) He provided the following principles as guides for the best type of management.

(a) *A large daily task:* each person in the establishment, high or low should have a clearly defined daily task.

(b) *Standard conditions:* the worker should be given such standardized conditions and appliances as will enable him to accomplish his/her task with certainty.

(c) *High pay for success:* the worker should be sure of high pay when she/he accomplished his task.

(d) *Loss in case of failure:* when a worker fails to be productive. She/he will be sure that sooner or later, she/he will be the loser for it.

From the above presentation, it can be stated that Taylor provided a base up on which much of our current thinking about management is established.

Classical Organisation Theory (Administrative Management Theory)

These ideas focused on the problems faced by top managers of large organisations. Since this branch of the classical approach (*classical* organisation theory) focused on the management of organisations while scientific management focused on the management of work. The two major purposes of *classical* organisation theory were to:

1. Develop basic principles that could guide the design, creation, and maintenance of large organisations and
2. Identify the basic functions of managing organisations.

It holds a functional approach to management-it grew out of the need to find guideline for managing complex organisations such as factories. Although, there were areas of overlap, a major distinction between the two schools of thought is that the Administration management theory (from the Managing Director or Chief Executive officer) and worked downwards on the organisation hierarchy, whereas the scientific management emphasised management at the operative level (Individuals at the workshop level). The administrative management theorists looked for common principles that characterised successful management.

Henry Fayol is acknowledged as the founder of the Administrative management school. He felt that sound administrative practices falls in to certain patterns that can be identified and analyzed. He presented "Principles of management" and "Functions of management"

Functions of Management

Fayol was perhaps the first individual to discuss management as a process with specific functions that all managers must perform. He believed that management should be taught. He called for the introduction of formal managerial training in schools. He proposed four management functions.

1. *Planning:* Fayol believed that managers must make the best possible forecast of events that could affect the organisation and draw up an operating plan to guide future decisions.
2. *Organising:* Fayol believed that managers must determine the appropriate combination of machines, material, and humans necessary to accomplish the task.
3. *Commanding:* In Fayol's scheme, commanding involved directing the activities of subordinates. He believed that managers should set a good example and have direct, two-way communication with subordinates. Finally managers must continually evaluate both the organisational structure and their subordinates, and they should not hesitate to change the structure if they consider it faulty, or to fire subordinates who are impotent.
4. *Controlling:* Controlling ensures that actual activities are consistent with planned activities.

Principles of Management

These principles that are fourteen in number that are forwarded by Fayol are also called classical principles of management: There are:

1. *Division of labour:* The more people specialise; the more efficiently they can perform their work.
2. *Authority:* Managers must give orders so that they can get things done.
3. *Discipline:* Members in an organisation need to respect the rules and agreements that govern the organisation.

4. *Unity of command* - each employee must receive instructions about a particular operation from only one person and also this employee should report to only superior (manager).
5. *Unity of direction* - those operations with in the organisation that have the same objective should be directed by only one manager using one plan.
6. *Subordination of individual interest to the common good:* In any undertaking, the interests of employees should not take precedence over the interests of the organisation as a whole.
7. *Remuneration* - compensation for work done should be fair to both employees and employers.
8. *Centralization* - decreasing the role of subordinates in decision-making is centralization; increasing their role is decentralization. He believed that managers should retain final responsibility but also need to give their subordinates enough authority.
9. *Hierarchy* - the line of authority showing the position head by organisational members from top to bottom.
10. *Order* - materials and people should be in the right place at the right time. People in particular should be in the jobs or position most suited for them.
11. *Equity* - managers should be both friendly and fair to their subordinates.
12. *Stability of staff* - a high employee turnover rate is not good for the efficient functioning of an organisation.
13. *Initiative* - subordinates should be given the freedom to conceive and carry out their plans.
14. *Esprit de corps* - promoting team spirit will give the organisation a sense of unity.

BEHAVIOURAL APPROACH

The behavioural approach to management developed partly because practising managers found that following the ideas of the classical approach did not achieve total efficiency and workplace harmony. The behavioural approach to management has two branches.

1. The *human relations approach* (was very popular in the 1940s and 1950s).
2. The *behavioural science approach* (became popular in the 1950s and still receives attention)

The Human Relations Approach

The classical school of thought ignored or underestimated the human factor in administration. The response to the perceived defects of the classical theory gave rise to the emergence of the human relations movement, which focus about people and their relationship in the organisation. The term human relation refers to the manner in which managers interact with subordinates. To develop good human relations, managers must know why their subordinates behave as they do and what psychological and social factors influence them. While scientific management concentrated on the physical environment of the job, human relations concentrated on the social environment

Human relations proponents believe that management should recognise the need of employees for recognition and social acceptance. Since groups provide members with feelings of acceptance and dignity, management should look upon the work group as a positive force, which could be utilised productively. Therefore, managers should be trained in people skills as well as in technical skills. Elton Mayo's research work on human relation movement is presented as follows.

Elton Mayo – is regarded as the founder of human relations movement. While mayo was at a the textile mill in Philadelphia, he addressed himself to workers problems- sore feet and legs resulting from standing on assembly line for ten hours or more. They held their work at low esteem and were depressed and pessimistic. He suggested the introduction of rest period to alleviate the sufferings of the workers and possibly improve productivity. While in Harvard, as an industrial psychologist, Mayo conducted series of studies at the Hawthorne plant. The purpose of these studies was to determine the effect of illumination on employee productivity. The intensity of the lighting was varied from fairly dark to bright and to very bright. The lighting in the control group remained the same.

In each instance, the productivity of the workers increased showing no relationship between the lighting and output. Instead of productivity going down when the intensity of the lighting was reduced, it went up. The researcher was surprised and justifiably believed that something other than illumination was responsible for the change in output of workers. The same experiment was tried with the rest period. There was no decline in productivity. When the rest period was decreased instead, productivity went up.

Consequently, it was concluded that social and psychological factors were responsible for the behaviour of the employees that resulted in high productivity. They knew that they were given special recognition and that this experiment was of special interest to the management and supervisors. Thus, something more than external environmental factors produced these results. The result of this experiment, which produced what is referred to as *"Hawthorne effect"* showed the effect which attitude towards work, management and work group have on human behaviour.

The Behavioural Science Approach

The individuals in the behavioural science branch of the behavioural approach believe that man is much more complex than the "economic man" description of the classical approach and the "social man" description of the human relations approach. The emphasis of the behavioural science approach concentrates more on the nature of work itself, and the degree to which it can fulfil the human need to use skills and abilities.

Behavioural scientists believe that an individual is motivated to work for many reasons in addition to making money and forming social relationships.

Managerial Science Approach

The management science approach is a modern version of early emphasis on the "management of work" by those interested in scientific management. Its key feature is the use of mathematics and statistics to aid in resolving production and operations problems. The approach focuses on solving technical rather than human behaviour problems. The management science approach has only existed formally for approximately 55 years. It began during the early part of World War II when England was confronted with some complex military problems that had never been faced before, such as antisubmarine warfare strategy. To try to solve these kinds of problems, the English formed teams of scientists, mathematicians, and physicists. The units were named *operations research* teams, and they proved to be extremely valuable. When the war was over, American business firms began to use the approach.

Today the operations research approach has been formalised and renamed the management science approach. Basically, it involves mixed teams of specialists from whatever fields the problem being attacked calls for. The team members analyse the problem and often develop a mathematical representation of it. Thus, they can change certain factors in the equations to see what would happen if such a change was actually made in the real world. The results of their work often become useful to management in making a final decision. One of their important purposes is to provide management with *quantitative bases* for decisions.

MODERN APPROACHES TO MANAGEMENT

There have been some attempts to aid managers in integrating the three approaches to management. The attempts include:

1. The *systems approach:* The systems approach stresses that organisations must be viewed as total systems with each part linked to every other part.
2. The *contingency approach:* The *contingency approach* stresses that the correctness of a managerial practice is contingent on how it fits the particular situation to which it is applied; in other words, it "depends on the situation." Let us briefly examine each approach.

The Systems Approach

The systems approach to management is essentially a way of thinking about organisations and management problems. The approach views an organisation as a group of interrelated parts with a unified purpose: surviving and ideally thriving in an environment. Thus, in solving problems, managers must view the organisation as a dynamic whole and try to anticipate the unintended as well as the intended impacts of their decisions.

From the systems perspective, management involves managing and solving problems in each part of the organisation but doing so with the understanding that actions taken in one part of the organisation affect other parts of the organisation. In solving problems, managers must view the organisation as a dynamic whole and try to anticipate the unintended as well as the intended impacts of their decisions. Today's organisations are generally considered open systems: that is, they are affected by environmental forces. A manager must be aware of those forces and must adapt the organisation to them. By viewing a firm as a single unit and as part of a large system, a manager will have better perspective when it comes to planning, organising, staffing, leading and controlling. With a systems perspective, managers can more easily achieve coordination between the objectives of the various parts of the organisation and the objectives of the organisation as a whole.

The Contingency Approach

The systems approach to management advocates that managers recognise that organisations are systems comprised of interdependent parts and that a change in one part affects other parts. It is useful for managers to see how the parts fit together. The contingency approach can help you better understand their interdependence.

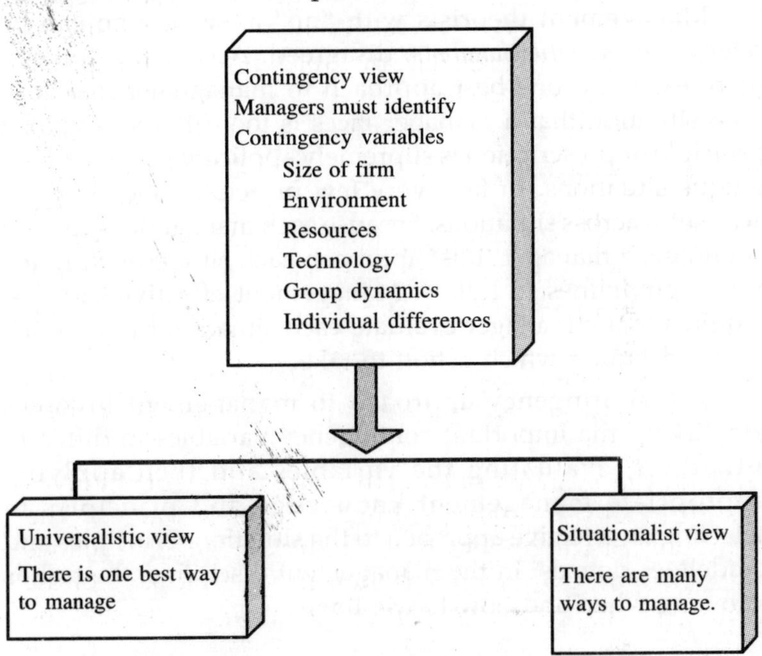

Fig. 2.1: **A Continuum of Views on Approaches to Management Effectiveness**

Source: Ivancevich, Donnelly and Gibson, Management: Principles and Functions; 4th Edition, Boston, 1989, p.18 USA.

To the question "Is there any "one best way" to apply management principles and to conduct the functions of management to achieve organisational effectiveness? Some management theorists are with a "yes" answer and some others are with "no" answer.

Management theorists with a "yes" answer advocated the "universalistic" view of management effectiveness. They argued that there indeed exists a one best way to perform different management functions. In their view, the task of management theorists is to identify these superior management prescriptions by developing and then testing theory via research.

Management theorists with "no" answer, who can be referred to as *situationalists,* disagreed. According to them, there exists no one best approach to management because each situation that a manager faces is too different. No one principle or prescription is supremely applicable across totally unique situations. In fact, very few principles and concepts are useful across situations. Because each managerial situation is unique, a manager must approach each situation with few if any guidelines to follow. Management effectiveness first requires that a manager evaluate each situation from scratch before deciding which action to take.

The contingency approach to management involves identifying the important contingency variables in different situations, evaluating the variables and then applying appropriate management knowledge and principles in selecting an effective approach to the situation. Principles and guidelines do exist in the management discipline; the task is knowing when and how to use them.

3 The Environment of Organisations

INTRODUCTION

We recall from the discussion of the systems approach in the previous chapter. One of the basic assumptions of the systems theory is that organisations are neither self-sufficient nor self-contained. Rather, they exchange resources with and are dependent upon the external environment, defined as all elements outside an organisation that are relevant to the operations of the organisation. Organisations take inputs (raw materials, money, labour, and energy from the external environment, transform them into outputs (products or services), and send them back as outputs to the external environment.

Managers and their organisations operate within a difficult and complex environment. The pressures and challenges posed by the ever changing internal and external environment in which managers operate does mean that managers must be:

1. Aware of what constitutes the elements of their business environment.
2. Able to respond to the forces of the environment, which inevitably impinge on the operations of the business.

WHAT DO YOU UNDERSTAND BY ENVIRONMENT?

Environment is defined here as the aggregate of social, cultural, economic, and physical conditions that influence the life of an individual, organisation, or community. No enterprise of any kind can operate in the absence of environmental constraints, or restrictions imposed by the organisation's surroundings.

To the question, what determines successful business performance? Two schools of thought attempt to answer this question from diametrically different viewpoints. The schools of thought are environmental determinism and organisational determinism.

1. School of thought that supports environmental determinism

Proponents of this school thought specially scholars in the field of industrial organisation argue that business performance fundamentally is affected by competition in this industry and claim that the firm cannot influence its environment. According to them business's success depends largely on how an organisation fits with its environment.

2. School of thought who supports organisational determinism

Scholars in sociology, economics, and strategic management believe that an organisation not only adapts to its environment but that the success of the business depends on how well it can influence the environmental forces in its favour.

Even though managers may be able to do little to influence the forces of the environment, they do not have any alternative but to respond to them. The issue is close to the hotly debated question of whether individuals affect their environment or whether the environment affects the individuals. 'The answer is "a little of both".

We can assume that environmental forces influence organisations. We also can accept the idea that firms can use the external environment to their own advantage. Managers are not expected only to react when there are changes in the environment but they should be able to anticipate the changes and take steps to prevent them. Organisations are accountable to a number of different groups, including customers, suppliers, creditors, government agencies, and the public. They must be responsive to these groups and operate within the boundaries they establish.

Managers don't have the luxury of being able to do what ever they choose. They must make decision within a framework of external and internal forces. The framework defines the environment of Management. These forces can be constraints or opportunities for an organisation. The relationship between the organisation (be it a business enterprise or a government organisation) and its environment can be examined in several ways. First the organisation can be viewed as importing various kinds of inputs such as human, capital, managerial and technical inputs as services and goods. These inputs are transformed to produce outputs (goods and/ or services). A second approach in the study of the relationship between the organisation and the society is to focus on the demands and legitimate rights of different claimants such as employees, consumers, suppliers, stockholders, government and community. A third approach is to view the organisation operating in an external environment of opportunities and constraints. No single approach is sufficient for all times and in all circumstances. They are complimentary; the elements external to the enterprise affect its performance as well as those elements with in the organisations.

Environmental influences can be of two general categories. They are:

1. External environment; and
2. Internal environment.

External Environment

Constraints that are categorised under external environment are those that are imposed from outside the organisation and are generally beyond the control of the organisation. Each of these forces, working independently or in combination with others, imposes constraints or creates opportunities for the firm. Schwartz 1984 discusses some of the major external constraints that may restrict managers in performing the functions of management as follows.

Political and Legal Forces

Legal-political constraints include such things as existing laws and regulations, taxes, and political stability. There are laws that regulate nearly every facet of human existence. Laws come about, generally, to prevent or stop the abuse of power. There are laws that regulate-working conditions, minimum wages, the safety of workers, the sale of stock, competitive practices, pricing, product safety, business location, fair hiring practices, and so on. Legal-political constraints have a major effect on decisions regarding the location of business. Managers of multinational companies are particularly concerned with political stability in deciding where to operate subsidiaries. With regard to legal-political constraints, managers can make inputs at the local, state, and national levels. Managers may testify, present evidence, lobby, or take other actions in an attempt to influence government decisions. What can be understood from the above discussion is that an organisation usually cannot influence what a government body does.

Constraints Imposed by Consumers

Consumers hold considerable power regarding what an organisation can and cannot do. The consuming public generally, by its purchases, decides what products (services) will succeed in the market.

Constraints Imposed by Competitors' Actions

A competitor, especially a leading one, through its actions places restrictions on what another organisation can do. Pricing decisions in many firms, for example often reflect the pricing decisions of a leading competitor. Or a competing firm may hold important patent and thus restrict other organisations' actions.

Constraints Imposed by Labour Unions

Through contracts negotiated with management, labour unions restrict what management may want to do in such areas as wages, vacations, retirement plans, working conditions, and employment policies.

Constraints Imposed by Education of Potential Employees

Educational constraints-such things as the level of education of the available work force and the availability of workers with appropriate skills have a direct effect on management. It would be extremely difficult, for example, to operate in a highly technical industry if there were few technically skilled people in the area.

Constraints Imposed by Society

Society ultimately establishes the laws and regulations under which all organisations operate. If a firm ignores social concerns regarding such matters as environmental protection, product safety, and unfair employment practices, society will react 'by imposing legal restrictions. In addition, the individual members of society impose restrictions on an organisation. Such sociological constraints include such matters as prevailing attitudes toward work, material gain, and change. Managing most enterprises is easier, for example, if employees have a strong work ethic than if they regard work as an unpleasant part of life.

Constraints Imposed by the Economy

The economic environment includes trends in the gross national product (GNP), disposable personal, income, consumer spending, industrial investment, employment, population growth, money markets, capital markets, the structure of industry, the nature of competition, demand for products, and similar variables. Business organisations are increasingly influenced by government-imposed economic policies. The Central Bank of Ethiopia, for example, has power over interest rates and the supply of money. All businesses would like to borrow money at very low interest rates. But the price they must pay for the money they require is not in their control. Rather it is determined by a number of complex factors. Economic constraints differ greatly among nations. Economic constraints also change. Interest rates, for example, may rise or fall significantly in a period of months in some countries.

Technological

One of the most pervasive factors in the environment is technology. It's science, which provides the knowledge, and it's technology that uses the knowledge. Technology includes invention, techniques and the vast store of organised knowledge about virtually everything.

Internal Environment

A business's environment is affected not only by external forces but also by internal forces. These include:

1. The physical, financial, and human resources of the firm.
2. The value systems of managers. Like external forces, these internal influences provide both problems and opportunities for the firm.

Physical Resources

Every firm has physical resource that either aid or hinder its performance. They include the physical plant and its location, manufacturing equipment, raw materials transportation and distribution facilities and other resources vital to its operations.

Financial Resources

A firms financial resources include the assets that enable it to meet its operating costs, expand, conduct research and development, borrow additional funds and so on. A businesses financial position affects its ability to take advantages of profitable opportunities when they arise. The financially sound firm can borrow money at lower interest rates, insist on special services as a highly valued customer, and maintain goodwill of suppliers, stockholders, creditors, and others. The financially unstable company, on the other hand, most likely will find it difficult to raise capital, maintain a highly competitive position or take advantage of income producing opportunities.

Human Resources

The resource that shapes firms character and differentiates it from other companies is its people. Although a company's human resources is not reflected on the balance sheet, people are just as important, perhaps most important, than its physical and financial resources. Human resources include blue-collar worker, technical and professional employees, staff support personnel, and managers. Especially important are people whose technical and professional expertise set the firm apart from its competitors. One of the most important human resources, however, is the organisation management. Managers who have the necessary technical, human, and conceptual skill belong to one of the most important asset of the organisation. Many companies have grown from very modest operation to giant economic powers because of effective management.

Human values are basic convictions about what is right and wrong. Managers, like all other people, operate within the scope and limitations of their moral convictions. Their value systems help define the firm's internal environment. Every manager has needs, ambitions, preferences, and desires. And every manager must make decisions that fulfil or detract from these needs and wants. Thus, a manager's decision making is shaped by his or her needs, desires, and moral beliefs, and by the expectations of the organisation (desires, wants, ambitions and preferences on one hand and organisational expectation and personal values on the other). Each of these forces, working independently or with others is reflected in what a manager does.

Classification of Organisations External Environment

It was discussed that three important factors i.e. types of managers, managerial skills, and managerial roles influence managerial behaviour and performance. We know the value of each of these factors will differ from situation to situation and manager to manager. Another factor influencing a manager's ability to perform is the external environment, a set of outside forces that are difficult to control. These factors may have a profound impact on how well a manager performs.

The following section outlines the broad impacts of environmental influences on the job of managing. This part of the discussion of environmental effects will focus on the different types of environments in which organisations compete. Ivancevich, Donnelly and Gibson (1989) classify organisation's environment as:

1. Turbulent environment;
2. Hostile environment;
3. Diverse, or Technically complex and are discussed as follows.

Such a classification will not only enhance our understanding of the different external forces on organisational performance but will let us learn how organisations react to the classified environment types.

A Turbulent Environment

An organisation in a turbulent environment faces rapid changes on a regular basis. These changes may come from technological innovations, changes in government regulations or economic or competitive shifts. Because lack of environmental stability, that is an extremely difficult environment to manage.

A Hostile Environment

When an organisation faces intense competition for customers, resources, or both, it is operating in a hostile environment

A Diverse Environment

An international organisation faces a diversity of languages, consumers, governments, cultures, and tastes. This diverse environment influences not only what the organisation does and how it does it, but when it makes certain moves, as well.

A Technically Complex Environment

The electronics, computer, and telecommunications industries operate in technically complex environments. They demand sophisticated information and the recruitment of highly technical personnel to survive. New developments can occur quickly, and present products can fast become obsolete as technological breakthroughs occur.

Managerial Responses to a Changing External Environment

Since an organisation must operate in a world that includes changing environmental forces, managers must respond to them. There are no sure methods of coping with environmental forces, but there are some that can be used with varying degrees of success. An organisation can attempt to change the external environmental forces in a way that is suitable to its needs and goals." Or, through its management team it can develop suitable internal responses for coping with the changes. Ivancevich, Donnelly and Gibson/1989/ describe a few of the internal response used to maintain and sustain performance by management.

Fire Fighting

The fire-fighting response to environmental forces means sitting back and letting things happen-and then dealing with the result." The problem with this type of response is that the external force-a problem or a competitor-may have become so big by the time the company reacts that any response is an uphill battle (very difficult battle).

Organisational Structure

As the complexity in the external environment increases, so does the complexity in organisational structure. Each force in the external environment requires an internal organisational response. For example, customers in the environment are the main responsibility of the marketing department within the organisation. Likewise, the technological changes and advancements in the environment are the responsibility of a research and development unit within the firm.

The Boundary Spanning Job

A boundary spanning job is one that links two or more systems in different organisations such as a firm and its external environment." The individual is a link between the organisations and the customer and can carry information and ideas back and forth between the firm and the environment. The boundary spanner serves two major purposes:

1. To detect and process information about changes in the external environment.
2. To represent the organisation to the public.

These functions are extremely important because they can provide data, suggestions, and ideas to decision makers who can use the information to devise and implement plans for coping.

Strategic Planning

Strategic Planning is a crucial managerial response to external environmental forces. Strategic planning may be defined, as is a management process that involves the determination of the basic long-term objectives of the organisation and the adoption of specific action plans for attaining these objectives. The five interrelated elements of strategic planning are:

1. Analysing the environment in terms of mission, threats, changes, and opportunities.
2. Establishing objectives.
3. Performing a situational analysis focusing on the external environmental forces that play the most significant role in the firms success.
4. Selecting the approaches (strategies) that will be used to accomplish the objectives.
5. Implementing and monitoring the actions necessary to accomplish the goals of the strategic plan.

Planning

MEANING AND DEFINITION

Planning is an intellectual and continuous managerial function and is the beginning of the process of management. In business and industry it is a very important management function; it involves major activities such as, setting goals, objectives, determining policies and making decisions.

Planning is the process of establishing goals and suitable courses of action for achieving these goals. It is the process of deciding in advance what is to be done, who is to do, how it is to be done, and when it is to be done.

George Terry: Planning is the selection and relating of facts and making and using of assumptions regarding the future in the visualisation and formation of proposed activities believed necessary to achieve desired results.

Allen: A plan is a trap laid to capture the future.

Koontz & O'Donnel: Planning is deciding in advance what to do, how to do it, when to do it and who is to do it. It bridges the gap from where we are and where we want to go.

NATURE AND IMPORTANCE

The nature of planning can be highlighted by examining its major aspects like:

(a) its contribution to purpose and objectives;

(b) its primacy among the managerial functions;

(c) its pervasiveness; and

(d) the efficiency of resulting plans.

The importance are: primacy of planning, focus on objectives, offset uncertainty and change, help in coordination and control and increase in organisational efficiency.

TYPES OF PLANS

Plan can be categorized into several types based on certain aspects. Plans can be classified as under:

1. *Hierarchical Plans:* Mission, vision, goals and objectives, policies, strategies, procedures, projects and programmes, budgets and reports.
2. *Time based:* Short range, medium range and long range plans.
3. *Functional:* Human resource planning, marketing plan, financial plan, materials planning, production plans.
4. *Level based:* Strategic, tactical and operational plans.
5. *Others:* Derivative, situational and contingency plans.

STEPS IN PLANNING PROCESS

The planning process is different from one type of plan to another. Because various factors that go into planning process may differ.

- *Step 1:* Perception/being aware of Opportunities – Perception and an awareness of opportunities in the external and internal environment is the real starting point of planning.
- *Step 2:* Establishing Objectives – At this stage, major organisational, departmental objectives are set.
- *Step 3:* Planning and developing Premises – After determination of objectives, the premises must be developed, i.e., the conditions under which planning activities will be undertaken. The external and internal environment as premises should be considered.

- *Step 4:* Forecasting & Budget – This stage would be for identifying, evaluating and selecting a course for preparing plans. Forecasting techniques will be used and budget will be prepared.
- *Step 5:* Formulating Derivative Plans – Next stage would be formulating derivative plans, which are supportive plans to the master plans.
- *Step 6:* Establishing sequence of activities – This is a sequencing or numberising plans by budgeting.
- *Step 7:* Implementation – After everything is over, the plan is ready to implement.

STRATEGIC PLANNING

Strategic planning is one specific type of planning. Strategies are the outcome of strategic planning. An organisation's strategies define the business the firm is in, the criteria for entering the business, and the basic actions the organisation will follow in conducting its business (Higgins, Page 229.) Strategies are major plans that commit large amounts of the organisation's resources to proposed actions, designed to achieve its major objectives and goals. Strategic planning is the process by which the organisation's strategies are determined. In the process, three basic questions are answered:

1. Where are we now?
2. Where do we want to be?
3. How do we get there?

The "where are we now?" question is answered through the first three steps of the strategy formulation process:

1. perform internal and external environmental analyses;
2. review vision, mission and objectives; and
3. determine SWOT: Strengths, Weaknesses, Opportunities and Threats. SWOT analysis requires managers to be honest, self-disciplined and thorough. Going on to strategy choices without a comprehensive SWOT analysis is risky.

Strengths and weaknesses come from the internal environment of the firm. Strengths can be exploited, built upon and made key to accomplishment of mission and objectives. Strengths reflect past accomplishments in production, financial, marketing and human resource management. Weaknesses are internal characteristics that have the potential to limit accomplishment of mission and objectives. Weaknesses may be so important that they need to be addressed before any further strategic planning steps are taken.

Opportunities and threats are uncontrollable by management because they are external to the firm. Opportunities provide the firm the possibility of a major improvement. Threats may stand in the way of a firm reaching its mission and objectives.

DECISION MAKING

Some Definitions

A good place to start is with some standard definitions of decision making.

1. *Decision making is the study of identifying and choosing alternatives based on the values and preferences of the decision maker.* Making a decision implies that there are alternative choices to be considered, and in such a case we want not only to identify as many of these alternatives as possible but to choose the one that:
   (a) has the highest probability of success or effectiveness; and
   (b) best fits with our goals, desires, lifestyle, values, and so on.
2. *Decision making is the process of sufficiently reducing uncertainty and doubt about alternatives to allow a reasonable choice to be made from among them.* This definition stresses the information-gathering function of decision making. It should be noted here that uncertainty is *reduced* rather than eliminated. Very few decisions are made with

absolute certainty because complete knowledge about all the alternatives is seldom possible. Thus, every decision involves a certain amount of risk.

Kinds of Decisions

There are several basic kinds of decisions.

1. *Decisions whether:* This is the yes/no, either/or decision that must be made before we proceed with the selection of an alternative. Should I buy a new TV? Should I travel this summer? Decisions whether are made by weighing reasons pro and con. The PMI technique discussed in the next chapter is ideal for this kind of decision.

   It is important to be aware of having made a decision whether, since too often we assume that decision making begins with the identification of alternatives, *assuming that the decision to choose one has already been made.*

2. *Decisions which:* These decisions involve a choice of one or more alternatives from among a set of possibilities, the choice being based on how well each alternative measures up to a set of predefined criteria.

3. *Contingent decisions:* These are decisions that have been made but put on hold until some condition is met.

Most people carry around a set of already made, contingent decisions, just waiting for the right conditions or opportunity to arise. Time, energy, price, availability, opportunity, encouragement—all these factors can figure into the necessary conditions that need to be met before we can act on our decision.

Decision Making is a Recursive Process

A critical factor that decision theorists sometimes neglect to emphasize is that in spite of the way the process is presented on paper, decision making is a nonlinear, recursive process. That is, most decisions are made by moving back and forth between the choice of criteria (the characteristics we want our choice to meet) and the identification of alternatives (the possibilities we can choose from among).

The alternatives available influence the criteria we apply to them, and similarly the criteria we establish influence the alternatives we will consider. Key point, then, is that the characteristics of the alternatives we discover will often revise the criteria we have previously identified.

The Components of Decision Making

The Decision Environment

Every decision is made within a decision environment, which is defined as the collection of information, alternatives, values, and preferences *available at the time of the decision.* An ideal decision environment would include all possible information, all of it accurate, and every possible alternative. However, both information and alternatives are constrained because the time and effort to gain information or identify alternatives are limited. The time constraint simply means that a decision must be made by a certain time. The effort constraint reflects the limits of manpower, money, and priorities. (You wouldn't want to spend three hours and half a tank of gas trying to find the very best parking place at the mall.) Since decisions must be made within this constrained environment, we can say that *the major challenge of decision making is uncertainty,* and a major goal of decision analysis is to reduce uncertainty. We can almost never have all information needed to make a decision with certainty, so most decisions involve an undeniable amount of risk.

The fact that decisions must be made within a limiting decision environment suggests two things. First, it explains why hindsight is so much more accurate and better at making decisions that foresight. As time passes, the decision environment continues to grow and expand. New information and new alternatives appear—even after the decision must be made. Armed with new information after the fact, the hindsighters can many times look back and make a much better decision than the original maker, *because the decision environment has continued to expand.*

The second thing suggested by the decision-within-an-environment idea follows from the above point. Since the decision environment continues to expand as time passes, it is often advisable to put off making a decision until close to the deadline. Information and alternatives continue to grow as time passes, so to have access to the most information and to the best alternatives, do not make the decision too soon. Now, since we are dealing with real life, it is obvious that some alternatives might no longer be available if too much time passes; that is a tension we have to work with, a tension that helps to shape the cutoff date for the decision.

Delaying a decision as long as reasonably possible, then, provides three benefits:

1. The decision environment will be larger, providing more information. There is also time for more thoughtful and extended analysis.
2. New alternatives might be recognized or created. Version 2.0 might be released.
3. The decision maker's preferences might change. With further thought, wisdom, and maturity, you may decide not to buy car X and instead to buy car Y.

The Effects of Quantity on Decision Making

Many decision makers have a tendency to seek more information than required to make a good decision. When too much information is sought and obtained, one or more of several problems can arise:

1. A delay in the decision occurs because of the time required to obtain and process the extra information. This delay could impair the effectiveness of the decision or solution.
2. Information overload will occur. In this state, so much information is available that decision-making ability actually declines because the information in its entirety can no longer be managed or assessed appropriately. A major problem caused by information overload is forgetfulness. When too much information is taken into

memory, especially in a short period of time, some of the information (often that received early on) will be pushed out.

The example is sometimes given of the man who spent the day at an information-heavy seminar. At the end of the day, he was not only unable to remember the first half of the seminar but he had also forgotten where he parked his car that morning.

3. Selective use of the information will occur. That is, the decision maker will choose from among all the information available only those facts which support a preconceived solution or position.
4 Mental fatigue occurs, which results in slower work or poor quality work.
5. Decision fatigue occurs, where the decision maker tires of making decisions. Often the result is fast, careless decisions or even decision paralysis—no decisions are made at all.

The quantity of information that can be processed by the human mind is limited. Unless information is consciously selected, processing will be biased toward the first part of the information received. After that, the mind tires and begins to ignore subsequent information or forget earlier information.

Decision Streams

A common misconception about decision making is that decisions are made in isolation from each other: you gather information, explore alternatives, and make a choice, without regard to anything that has gone before. The fact is, decisions are made in a context of other decisions. The typical metaphor used to explain this is that of a stream. There is a stream of decisions surrounding a given decision, many decisions made earlier have led up to this decision and made it both possible and limited. Many other decisions will follow from it.

Another way to describe this situation is to say that most decisions involve a choice from a group of preselected alternatives, made available to us from the universe of alternatives by the previous decisions we have made. Previous decisions have "activated" or "made operable" certain alternatives and "deactivated" or "made inoperable" others.

For example, when you decide to go to the park, your decision has been enabled by many previous decisions. You had to decide to live near the park; you had to decide to buy a car or learn about bus routes and so on. And your previous decisions have constrained your subsequent ones: you can't decide to go to a park this afternoon if it is three states away. By deciding to live where you do, you have both enabled and disabled a whole series of other decisions.

We might say, then, that every decision:

1. follows from previous decisions;
2. enables many future decisions; and
3. prevents other future decisions.

People who have trouble making decisions are sometimes trapped by the constraining nature of decision making. Every decision you make precludes other decisions, and therefore might be said to cause a loss of freedom. If you decide to marry Terry, you no longer can decide to marry Shawn. However, just as making a decision causes a loss of freedom, it also creates new freedom, new choices and new possibilities. So making a decision is liberating as well as constraining. And a decision left unmade will often result in a decision by default or a decision being made for you.

It is important to realise that every decision you make affects the decision stream and the collections of alternatives available to you both immediately and in the future. In other words, decisions have far reaching consequences.

Concepts and Definitions

1. *Information:* This is knowledge about the decision, the effects of its alternatives, the probability of each alternative, and so forth. A major point to make here is that while substantial information is desirable, the statement that "the more information, the better" is not true. Too much information can actually reduce the quality

of a decision. See the discussion on The Effects of Quantity on Decision Making above.

2. *Alternatives:* These are the possibilities one has to choose from. Alternatives can be identified (that is, searched for and located) or even developed (created where they did not previously exist). Merely searching for preexisting alternatives will result in less effective decision making.
3. *Criteria:* These are the characteristics or requirements that each alternative must possess to a greater or lesser extent. Usually the alternatives are rated on how well they possess each criterion. For example, alternative Toyota ranks an 8 on the criterion of economy, while alternative Buick ranks a 6 on the same criterion.
4. *Goals:* What is it you want to accomplish? Strangely enough, many decision makers collect a bunch of alternatives (say cars to buy or people to marry) and then ask, "Which should I choose?" without thinking first of what their goals are, what overall objective they want to achieve. Next time you find yourself asking, "What should I do? What should I choose?" ask yourself first, "What are my goals?"

   A component of goal identification should be included in every instance of decision analysis.
5. *Value:* Value refers to how desirable a particular outcome is, the value of the alternative, whether in dollars, satisfaction, or other benefit.
6. *Preferences:* These reflect the philosophy and moral hierarchy of the decision maker. We could say that they are the decision maker's "values," but that might be confusing with the other use of the word, above. If we could use that word here, we would say that personal values dictate preferences. Some people prefer excitement to calmness, certainty to risk, efficiency to esthetics, quality to quantity, and so on. Thus, when one person chooses to ride the wildest roller coaster in the park and another chooses a mild ride, both may be making good decisions, if based on their individual preferences.

7. *Decision Quality:* This is a rating of whether a decision is good or bad. A good decision is a logical one based on the available information and reflecting the preferences of the decision maker.

   The important concept to grasp here is that the quality of a decision is not related to its outcome: a good decision can have either a good or a bad outcome. Similarly, a bad decision (one not based on adequate information or not reflecting the decision maker's preferences) can still have a good outcome.

   For example, if you do extensive analysis and carefully decide on a certain investment based on what you know about its risks and your preferences, then your decision is a good one, even though you may lose money on the investment. Similarly, if you throw a dart at a listing of stocks and buy the one the dart hits, your decision is a bad one, even though the stock may go up in value.

   Good decisions that result in bad outcomes should thus not be cause for guilt or recrimination. If you decide to take the scenic route based on what you know of the road (reasonably safe, not heavily traveled) and your preferences (minimal risk, prefer scenery over early arrival), then your decision is a good one, even though you might happen to get in an accident, or have a flat tire in the middle of nowhere. It is not justified to say, "Well, this was a bad decision."

   In judging the quality of a decision, in addition to the concerns of logic, use of information and alternatives, three other considerations come into play:

   (a) *The decision must meet the stated objectives most thoroughly and completely.* How well does the alternative chosen meet the goals identified?

   (b) *The decision must meet the stated objectives most efficiently, with concern over cost, energy, side effects.* Are there negative consequences to the alternative that make that choice less desirable? We sometimes overlook this consideration in our search for thrills.

(c) *The decision must take into account valuable byproducts or indirect advantages.* A new employee candidate may also have extra abilities not directly related to the job but valuable to the company nonetheless. These should be taken into account.

8. *Acceptance:* Those who must implement the decision or who will be affected by it must accept it both intellectually and emotionally.

Acceptance is a critical factor because it occasionally conflicts with one of the quality criteria. In such cases, the best thing to do may be to choose a lesser quality solution that has greater acceptance.

Thus, the inferior method may produce greater results if the inferior one has greater support. One of the most important considerations in decision making, then, is the people factor. Always consider a decision in light of the people implementation.

A decision that may be technologically brilliant but that is sociologically stupid will not work. Only decisions that are implemented, and implemented with thoroughness (and preferably enthusiasm) will work the way they are intended to.

Approaches to Decision Making

There are two major approaches to decision making in an organisation, the authoritarian method in which an executive figure makes a decision for the group and the group method in which the group decides what to do.

1. *Authoritarian:* The manager makes the decision based on the knowledge he can gather. He then must explain the decision to the group and gain their acceptance of it. In some studies, the time breakdown for a typical operating decision is something like this:
   - make decision, 5 min.; explain decision, 30 min.; gain acceptance, 30 min.
2. *Group:* The group shares ideas and analyses, and agrees upon a decision to implement. Studies show that the

group often has values, feelings, and reactions quite different from those the manager supposes they have. No one knows the group and its tastes and preferences as well as the group itself. And, interestingly, the time breakdown is something like this:

- Group makes decision, 30 min.; explain decision, 0 min.; gain acceptance, 0 min.

Clearly, just from an efficiency standpoint, group decision making is better. More than this, it has been shown many times that *people prefer to implement the ideas they themselves think of.* They will work harder and more energetically to implement their own idea than they would to implement an idea imposed on them by others. We all have a love for our own ideas and solutions, and we will always work harder on a solution supported by our own vision and our own ego than we will on a solution we have little creative involvement with.

There are two types of group decision making sessions. First is free discussion in which the problem is simply put on the table for the group to talk about. For example, Joe has been offered a job change from shift supervisor to maintenance foreman. Should he take the job?

The other kind of group decision making is developmental discussion or structured discussion. Here the problem is broken down into steps, smaller parts with specific goals. For example, instead of asking generally whether Joe should take the job, the group works on sub questions: What are Joe's skills? What skills does the new job require? How does Joe rate on each of the skills required? Notice that these questions seek specific information rather than more general impressionistic opinions.

Developmental discussion:

1. insures systematic coverage of a topic; and
2. insures that all members of the group are talking about the same aspect of the problem at the same time.

Some Decision Making Strategies

As you know, there are often many solutions to a given problem, and the decision maker's task is to choose one of them. The task of choosing can be as simple or as complex as the importance of the decision warrants, and the number and quality of alternatives can also be adjusted according to importance, time, resources and so on. There are several strategies used for choosing. Among them are the following:

1. *Optimising:* This is the strategy of choosing the best possible solution to the problem, discovering as many alternatives as possible and choosing the very best. How thoroughly optimising can be done is dependent on:
   (a) importance of the problem
   (b) time available for solving it
   (c) cost involved with alternative solutions
   (d) availability of resources, knowledge
   (e) personal psychology, values

   Note that the collection of complete information and the consideration of all alternatives is seldom possible for most major decisions, so that limitations must be placed on alternatives.
2. *Satisficing:* In this strategy, the first satisfactory alternative is chosen rather than the best alternative. If you are very hungry, you might choose to stop at the first decent looking restaurant in the next town rather than attempting to choose the best restaurant from among all (the optimising strategy). The word *satisficing* was coined by combining *satisfactory* and *sufficient*. For many small decisions, such as where to park, what to drink, which pen to use, which tie to wear, and so on, the satisficing strategy is perfect.
3. *Maximax:* This stands for "maximise the maximums." This strategy focuses on evaluating and then choosing the alternatives based on their maximum possible payoff. This is sometimes described as the strategy of the

optimist, because favorable outcomes and high potentials are the areas of concern. It is a good strategy for use when risk taking is most acceptable, when the go-for-broke philosophy is reigning freely.

4. *Maximin:* This stands for "maximise the minimums." In this strategy, that of the pessimist, the worst possible outcome of each decision is considered and the decision with the highest minimum is chosen. The Maximin orientation is good when the consequences of a failed decision are particularly harmful or undesirable. Maximin concentrates on the salvage value of a decision, or of the guaranteed return of the decision. It's the philosophy behind the saying, "A bird in the hand is worth two in the bush."

Quiz shows exploit the uncertainty many people feel when they are not quite sure whether to go with a maximax strategy or a maximin one: "Okay, Mrs. Freen, you can now choose to take what you've already won and go home, or risk losing it all and find out what's behind door number three."

Example: I could put my $10,000 in a genetic engineering company, and if it creates and patents a new bacteria that helps plants resist frost, I could make $50,000. But I could also lose the whole $10,000. But if I invest in a soap company, I might make only $20,000, but if the company goes completely broke and gets liquidated, I'll still get back $7,000 of my investment, based on its book value.

Example: It's fourth down and ten yards to go on your twenty yard line. Do you go for a long pass or punt? Maximax would be to pass; Maximin would be to punt.

Decision Making Procedure

As you read this procedure, remember our discussion earlier about the recursive nature of decision making. In a typical decision making situation, as you move from step to step here, you will probably find yourself moving back and forth also.

1. *Identify the decision to be made together with the goals it should achieve:* Determine the scope and limitations of the

decision. Is the new job to be permanent or temporary or is that not yet known (thus requiring another decision later)? Is the new package for the product to be put into all markets or just into a test market? How might the scope of the decision be changed—that is, what are its possible parameters?

When thinking about the decision, be sure to include a clarification of goals: We must decide whom to hire for our new secretary, *one who will be able to create an efficient and organised office.* Or, We must decide where to go on vacation, *where we can relax and get some rest from the fast pace of society.*

2. *Get the facts:* But remember that you cannot get all the facts. Get as many facts as possible about a *decision within the limits of time imposed on you and your ability to process them,* but remember that virtually every decision must be made in partial ignorance. Lack of complete information must not be allowed to paralyse your decision. A decision based on partial knowledge is usually better than not making the decision when a decision is really needed. The proverb that "any decision is better than no decision," while perhaps extreme, shows the importance of choosing. When you are racing toward a bridge support, you must decide to turn away to the right or to the left. Which way you turn is less important than the fact that you do indeed turn.

   As part of your collection of facts, list your feelings, hunches, and intuitive urges. Many decisions must ultimately rely on or be influenced by intuition because of the remaining degree of uncertainty involved in the situation.

   Also as part of your collection of facts, consult those who will be affected by and who will have to implement your decision. Input from these people not only helps supply you with information and help in making the decision but it begins to produce the acceptance necessary in the implementers because they feel that they are part of the decision making process. As Russell Ackoff noted in *The Art of Problem Solving*, not consulting people involved in a decision is often perceived as an act of aggression.

3. *Develop alternatives:* Make a list of all the possible choices you have, including the choice of doing nothing. Not choosing one of the candidates or one of the building sites is in itself a decision. Often a non decision is harmful as we mentioned above—not choosing to turn either right or left is to choose to drive into the bridge. But sometimes the decision to do nothing is useful or at least better than the alternatives, so it should always be consciously included in the decision making process.

   Also be sure to think about not just identifying available alternatives but creating alternatives that don't yet exist. *For example, if you want to choose which major to pursue in college, think not only of the available ones in the catalog, but of designing your own course of study.*

4. *Rate each alternative:* This is the evaluation of the value of each alternative. Consider the negative of each alternative (cost, consequences, problems created, time needed, etc.) and the positive of each (money saved, time saved, added creativity or happiness to company or employees, etc.). Remember here that the alternative that you might like best or that would in the best of all possible worlds be an obvious choice will, however, not be functional in the real world because of too much cost, time, or lack of acceptance by others.

   Also don't forget to include indirect factors in the rating. If you are deciding between machines X, Y, and Z and you already have an employee who knows how to operate machine Z, that fact should be considered. If you are choosing an investigative team to send to Japan to look at plant sites and you have very qualified candidates A, B, and C, the fact that B is a very fast typist, a superior photographer or has some other side benefit in addition to being a qualified team member, should be considered. In fact, what you put on your hobbies and interests line on your resume can be quite important when you apply for a job just because employers are interested in getting people with a good collection of additional abilities.

5. *Rate the risk of each alternative:* In problem solving, you hunt around for a solution that best solves a particular problem, and by such a hunt you are pretty sure that the solution will work. In decision making, however, there is always some degree of uncertainty in any choice. Will Bill really work out as the new supervisor? If we decide to expand into Canada, will our sales and profits really increase? If we let Jane date Fred at age fifteen, will the experience be good? If you decide to marry person X or buy car Y or go to school Z, will that be the best or at least a successful choice?

   Risks can be rated as percentages, ratios, rankings, grades or in any other form that allows them to be compared. See the section on risk evaluation for more details on risking.

6. *Make the decision:* If you are making an individual decision, apply your preferences (which may take into account the preferences of others). Choose the path to follow, whether it includes one of the alternatives, more than one of them (a multiple decision) or the decision to choose none.

And of course, don't forget to implement the decision and then evaluate the implementation, just as you would in a problem solving experience.

One important item often overlooked in implementation is that when explaining the decision to those involved in carrying it out or those who will be affected by it, don't just list the projected benefits: frankly explain the risks and the drawbacks involved and tell why you believe the proposed benefits outweigh the negatives. Implementers are much more willing to support decisions when they:

1. understand the risks; and
2. believe that they are being treated with honesty and like adults.

Remember also that very few decisions are irrevocable. Don't cancel a decision prematurely because many new plans require time to work—it may take years for your new branch office in Paris to get profitable—but don't hesitate to change directions if a particular decision clearly is not working out or is being somehow harmful. You can always make another decision to do something else.

MANAGERIAL DECISION MAKING

This section focuses on the decision-making aspects of planning. Planning, in many respects, is decision-making. Planning involves deciding which objectives to set, which forecasting method to use, which strategies to apply to each objective, how much and what types of resources should be budgeted, and which policies are appropriate. A manager is continually making decisions throughout each stage of planning, and the quality of plans is determined in large part by the decision-making skills of managers.

Types of Decisions

Although managers in large business organisations, government offices, hospitals, and schools may be separated by background, lifestyle, and distance, they all sooner or later must share the common experience of making decisions. They all will face situations involving several alternatives and an evaluation of the outcome. Not all decisions are so monumental or time consuming. However, several authors believe that there are two types of decision situations-, "programmed" and "nonprogrammed " managers to solve problems.

Programmed Decisions

Programmed decisions are the decisions managers make in response to repetitive and routine problems. These decisions are "Programmable" because a specific procedure can be worked out to resolve them based on experience in similar situations. Once a standard Procedure has been established, it can be used to treat all like situations. If a particular situation occurs often, managers will develop a routine procedure for handling it.

Programmed decisions usually involve an organisation's everyday operational and administrative activities. They all found primarily at the middle and lower levels of management. Data used in making a programmed decision usually are complete and well defined. Participants know the details and agree on how to resolve the problem. Senior-level management usually is not involved with particular decisions like this, but may be interested in the results of a series of such decisions over a period of time.

Nonprogrammed Decisions

When a problem has not arisen in exactly the same manner before, or is complex or extremely important, it may require a *nonprogrammed decision*. Decisions are termed *nonprogrammed* when they are made for novel and unstructured problems. Making such decisions is clearly a creative process.

Nonprogrammed decisions are used to resolve nonrecurring problems. No well-established Procedure exists for handling them all. Primarily because in contrast to Programmed decisions, available data are usually incomplete Moreover, people involved in the decision making process may disagree on how the situation should be handled. Nonprograrmmed decisions are commonly found at the middle and top levels of management and often are related to an organisation's policy-making activities. Whether to add a product to the existing product line or to acquire another firm are examples of nonprogammed decisions.

Types of Decisions and Level of Management

Problems that arise infrequently and have a great deal of uncertainty surrounding them are often of a strategic nature and should be the concern of top management. Problems that arise frequently and have fairly certain outcomes should be the concern of lower levels of management. Middle managers in most organisations concentrate mostly on programmed decisions. Factors such as the nature of the problem, how frequently it arises, and the degree of certainty surrounding it should dictate at what level of management the decision should be made.

Decision Making Under Different-Conditions

Another labelling scheme for decision-making is to classify decisions according to the likelihood of the outcome, which often is determined by existing conditions.

This approach distinguishes three different types of decisions:

1. Decisions under certainty.
2. Decisions under risk.
3. Decisions under uncertainty.

Decisions Under Certainty

Decisions under certainty are those in which the external conditions are identified and very predictable. Decision making under certainty seldom occurs, however, because external conditions seldom are perfectly predictable and because it is impossible to try to account for all possible influences on any given outcome. A certainty situation means that a perfectly accurate decision will be made time after time. Of course, decision making under certainty is rare.

Decisions Under Risk

Decisions under risk are those in which probabilities can be assigned to the expected outcomes of each alternative. These probabilities are determined either objectively or subjectively.

Objective probability: The assignment of an objective probability is derived through historical data or past experience. In many cases, historical evidence is not available.

Subjective probability: The fact that in many cases, historical evidence is not available, a manager must rely on a personal estimate, or *subjective* probability, of the situation outcome. Even a manager who is able to estimate the likelihood that the various states of nature will occur faces risk conditions. A risk situation requires the use of probability estimates. The ability to estimate may be due to experience, incomplete but reliable information, or intelligence. Subjective probability is derived through knowledge of the subject.

Decisions Under Uncertainty

In decisions under uncertainty, probabilities cannot be assigned to surrounding conditions. Some conditions that are uncontrollable by management include competition, government regulations, technological advances, changes in the overall economy, and the social and cultural tendencies of society. To deal with uncertainty, the decision maker must be careful not to focus on a symptom, but must discover root causes. Unless the basic cause is discovered and acted on properly, the solution will not be long lasting. Uncertainty is associated with the consequences of alternatives, not the alternatives themselves. With this in mind, managers must devise a common method of measuring the consequences. Managers' attitudes toward risk influence the way they make decisions under uncertain conditions. A conservative person who is wary of taking risks probably would concentrate on the possible adverse outcomes in choosing alternatives. Someone with a more open risk-taking attitude most likely would stress the possible beneficial outcomes in a decision.

The Process of Decision Making

Decision making is not a fixed procedure, but it is a sequential process.' In most decision situations, managers go through a number of stages that help them think through the problem and develop alternative strategies. The stages need not be rigidly applied; their value lies in their ability to force the decision maker to structure the problem in a meaningful way. The stages for the decision making process include the following.

1. *Identify and define the problem:* The manager must then identify and define the problem and make some kind of decision to solve the problem. Identifying problems is not as easy as it may seem. If the problem is incorrectly identified or defined, any decisions made will be directed toward solving the wrong Problem. There are several criteria managers use to locate problems:

(a) *Deviation from past performance:* A sudden change in some established pattern of performance often indicates that a problem has developed.

(b) *Deviation from the plan:* When results do not meet planned objectives, a problem is likely.

(c) *Outside criticism:* Outsiders may identify problems customers may be dissatisfied with a new product or with their delivery schedules.

2. *Develop alternative solutions:* Once the manager has clearly defined the problem, it will be necessary to *develop* a number of *alternative* solutions-potential strategies or solutions to the problem.
3. *Evaluate alternative solutions for certain conditions, uncertain conditions and risk conditions:* The manager would have to *evaluate* each of the *alternative solutions.* Evaluation involves measuring and comparing the potential payoffs and possible consequences of each alternative solution.
4. *Select the alternative. A manager selects a strategy to solve a problem and to achieve predetermined objectives:* This point is most important. A decision is not an end in itself but only a *means* to an end. A decision also is not an isolated act. Therefore a manager should not forget the factors that lead up to the decision and a manager should not ignore the factors that follow the decision also, such as implementation and evaluation.
5. *Implement decision. Once the alternative is selected, the decision must be implemented:* A planning decision is useless unless the chosen strategy is implemented, and the choice must be implemented effectively to achieve the objectives for which it was made. A decision is only an abstraction if it is not implemented. It is possible that a "good" decision can be damaged by poor implementation. Thus, implementation may be just as important as the actual activity of selecting an alternative.
6. *Evaluate and control:* The management function of control involves comparing actual performance with the

performance specified in the objectives. Setting measurable objectives important. When measurable objectives do not exist, there is no way to judge performance. The manager would have to continue periodic measurement i.e., compare the results with the established standard, and if problems still exist, face new decisions.

Remember that the stages of the decision-making process listed will be helpful to develop your own list of stages for the decision-making process. The above process is more applicable to nonprogrammed decisions than to programmed decisions. Problems that occur infrequently, with a great deal of uncertainty surrounding the outcome require the manager to utilize the entire process. In contrast, problems that occur frequently are often handled by policies or rules, so it not necessary to develop and evaluate alternatives each time these problems arise.

Group Decision Making

Decisions making by individuals in an organisation was discussed. In most organisations, however, a great deal of decision making is achieved through committees, teams, task forces, and other kinds of groups. This is because managers frequently face situations in which they must seek and combine judgments in group meetings. This is especially true for nonprogrammed problems, which are novel, with much uncertainty regarding, the outcome. In most organisations, it is unusual to find decisions on such problems being made by one individual on a regular basis. The increased complexity of many of these problems requires specialised knowledge in numerous fields, usually not possessed by one person. This requirement, coupled with the reality that the decisions made must eventually be accepted and implemented by many units throughout the organisation, has increased the use of the collective approach to the decision-making process. The result for many managers has been an endless amount of time spent in meetings of committees and other groups. It has been found that many managers spend as much as 80 percent of their working time in committee meetings.

Groups usually take more time to reach a decision than individuals do, but bringing together individual specialists and experts has its benefits since the mutually reinforcing impact of their interaction results in better decisions.

Management by Objectives (MBO)

- *Management:* Getting things done through others. Management can simply be defined as managing men tactfully to achieve the organisation objectives.
- *Objectives:* Objectives are the ends through which enterprise activities are aimed – the end points of planning.
- *Objectives Hierarchy:* The objective hierarchy is presented in the following diagram. The overall organisation objective is to be achieved through the department and individual objectives.

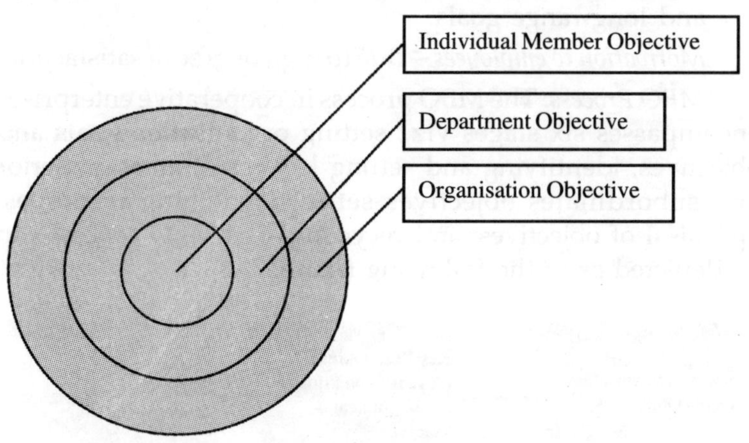

Fig. 4.1

Management by Objective (MBO): MBO is a new practice around the world. Some still think of it as an appraisal tool; others see it as a motivational technique; still others consider it as planning and control device.

Peter Drucker who first used this concept defined as, "management by objectives tells a manager what he ought to do. The proper organisation of this job enables him to do it. It is the spirit of the organisation that determines whether he will do it".

Features of MBO: The features of MBO are:

- *An approach* – A way of thinking about management and a collection of techniques.
- *Objective orientation* – It is the essence of MBO.
- *Participation of managers* – In objective settings and performance review.
- *Periodic review* – Regular review once a year (defining and modifying).
- *Provides guidelines* – For system and procedure, and resource allocation/delegation of authority.
- *Goal integration* – The individual, department and organisational goals are integrated as also the short-range and long-range goals.
- *Motivation to employees* – Due to high degree of satisfaction.

MBO Process: The MBO process in cooperative enterprises encompasses six stages viz., setting organisation goals and objectives, identifying and setting key result areas, superior and subordinates objectives setting, matching resources, appraisal of objectives, and recycling. The MBO process can be depicted as in the following figure.

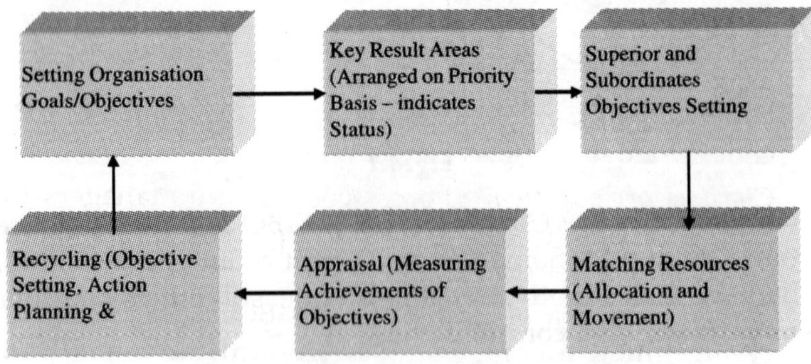

***Fig. 4.2:* MBO Process in Cooperatives**

The MBO process involved the above steps. In cooperatives first the organisation objectives are framed by the members at the initial stage at the time of organising the cooperative enterprise. They frame the objectives of the organisation in line with the cooperative values and principles. After framing the objective the members along with the executives identify the key result areas by arranging the activities and areas on priority basis. This indicates the strength and the present state of the cooperative enterprise. The next step is setting up of superior – subordinates objectives. In the management hierarchy the superior and subordinates objectives are framed. At this stage the subordinate objectives are taken into consideration while framing the superior objectives. Participatory approach is adopted at this stage. After framing the superior/subordinate objectives, the cooperative should go for matching the resources with the set objectives. Allocation of resources and movement of resources to various wings are done at this stage. At the stage of appraisal the objectives set are to be appraised by measuring the achievements made through the objectives. At the final stage of MBO process, proper recycling process is done time and again in order to cope up with the changes in the market environment. Here the recycling is done in line with objective setting; action planning and performance review is also undertaken.

Benefits of MBO: The following are the benefits of MBO in cooperatives.

- *Better managing* – MBO helps the cooperatives to have better management system and enables the members to concentrate on objective achievement.
- *Clarified organisation* – Forces cooperative managers to clarify the organisation goals and organisation structure based on the set objectives.
- *Personal commitment & satisfaction* – MBO leads to personal commitment among members, board members and employees and they get satisfaction.

- *Basis for organisation change* – MBO is the basis for cooperative organisation change. It supports the cooperatives to change their business techniques to survive and sustain the competitive business environment.
- *Development of effective control system* – Effective planning and control system is possible by having the concept of MBO in cooperative enterprises.

Organising

CONCEPT OF ORGANISATION

The organising function of management naturally and logically follows the planning function. As we have seen, managers decide what they want to accomplish in the way of profit, return on investment, students graduated, or whatever performance measures are appropriate objectives for the type of institution they are managing. But before these objectives can be accomplished, somebody must do some work. Not only must people do some work, they must do the right work. And that brings us to the organising function, because it is through the organising function that managers decide how the strategy and planned objective will be accomplished.

Another purpose of organising function is to achieve coordinated effort through the design of a structure of task and authority relationships. The two key works are design and structure. Design in this context implies that, managers make a conscious effort to predetermine the way employees do their work. Structure refers to relatively stable relationships and processes of the organisation. Organisational structure is considered by many to be "the anatomy of the organisation, providing a foundation within which the organisation functions. Thus, the structure of an organisation can be viewed as a framework. The idea of structure as a framework focuses on differentiation of positions, formulations of rules and procedures and prescriptions of authority. Thus, the purpose of structure is to regulate, or at least reduce, uncertainty in the behaviour of individual employees".

Organising is the management function that establishes relationships between activity and authority. It has four distinct activities:

1. It determines what work activities have to be done to accomplish organisational objectives.
2. It classifies the type of work needed and groups the work into manageable work units.
3. It assigns the work to individuals and delegates the appropriate authority.
4. It designs a hierarchy of decision-making relationships.

ORGANISATION STRUCTURE

From a managerial perspective, an effective organisational structure accomplishes several purposes.

1. It makes clear who is supposed to do a particular job or perform a task. In other words the organisational structure clarifies who is responsible.
2. It clarifies who is accountable to whom. It indicates who is in charge and who has the authority.
3. It clarifies the channels of communication. Communications flow between defined jobs and the principle of "need to know" determines who should be included in the channel.
4. An effective organisational structure will enable managers to allocate resources to the objectives defined in the planning process.

Organisation Chart Showing the Organisation Structure

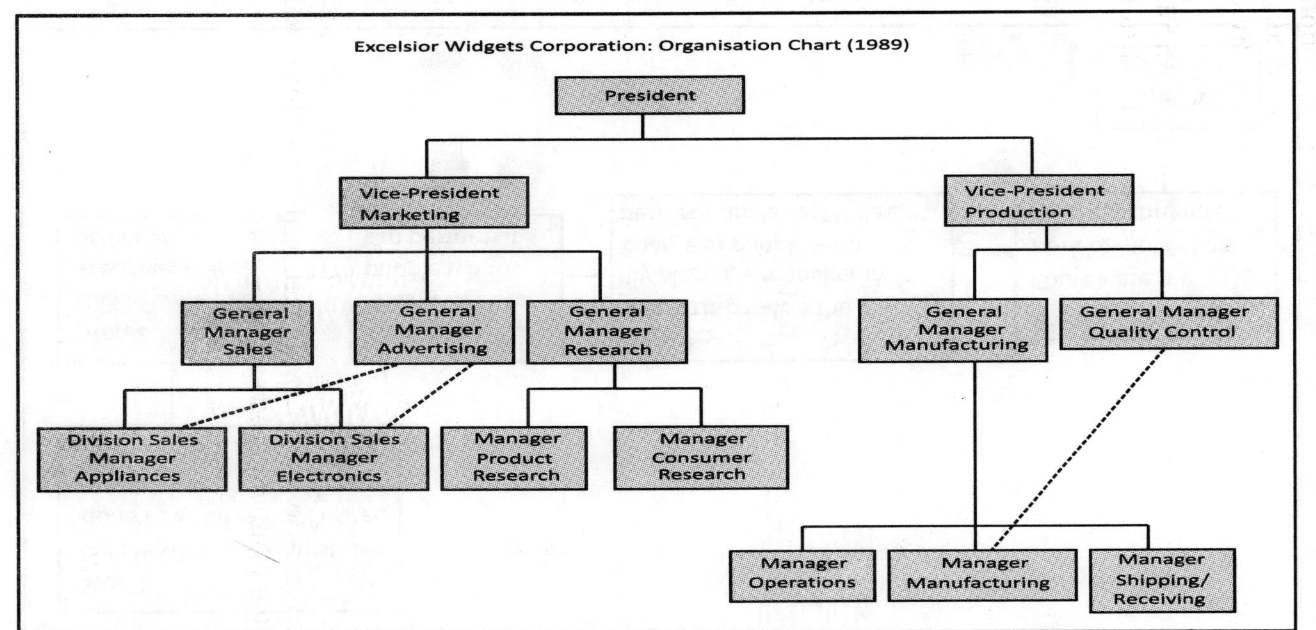

Source: Plunkett, Warren R., and Attner, Raymond F., Introduction to Management; USA Kent Publishing Co. Boston, 1989 p. 195, USA.

Illustration of the Organising Function as a Five-step Process

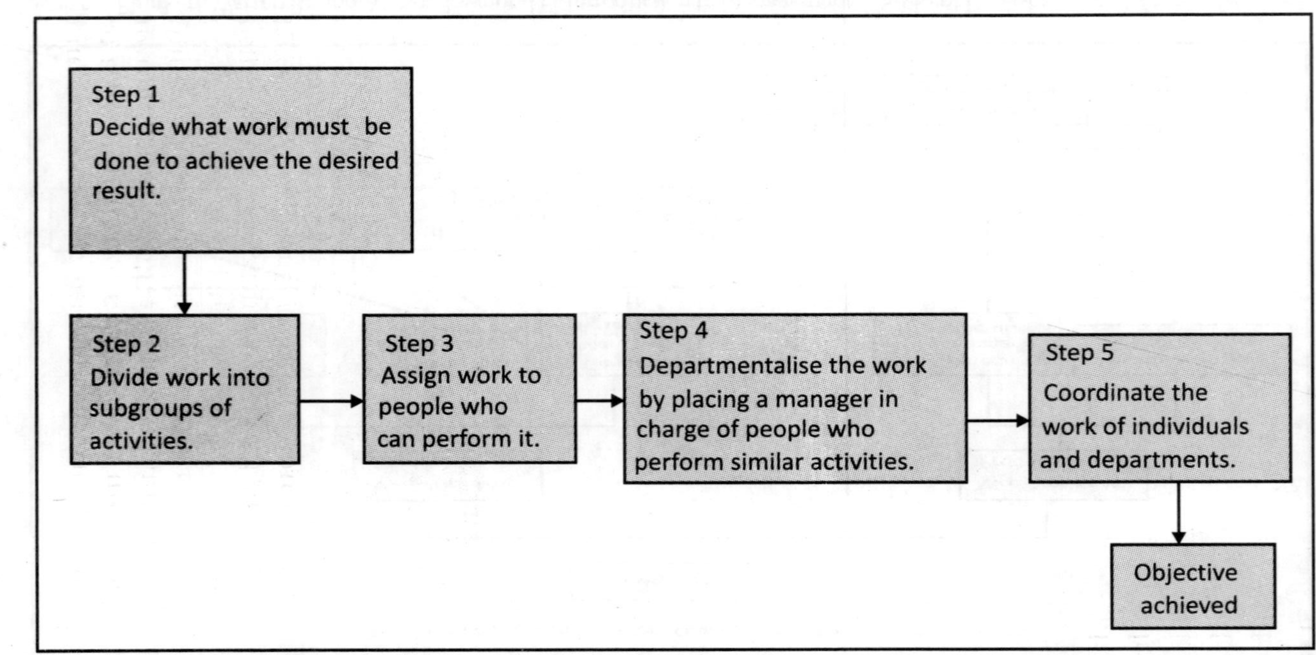

Source: Schwartz, David, Introduction to Management: Principles, Practices, and Processes, New York: Harcourt Brace Jovanovich, Inc., 1980, p. 210 USA

Principles of Organisation

- Principle of definition.
- Principle of objective.
- Principle of specialisation or division of work.
- Principle of coordination.
- Principle of authority.
- Principle of responsibility.
- Principle of efficiency.
- Principle of uniformity.
- Principle of correspondence.
- Principle of unity of command.
- Principle of balance.
- Principle of span of control.
- Principle of flexibility.
- Principle of scalar chain.

FORMAL AND INFORMAL ORGANISATION/GROUPS

As noted previously, structured organisations consist of two kinds of groups. One is the formal group, which is created by management. A formal group has several prescribed characteristics: it has a designated or appointed leader, a specific mission or assignment, imposed rules, specified performance standards, and known rewards and punishment.

A committee is an example of a formal group. It has a chairperson, a reason or purpose for existing, rules to follow in performing its mission, certain standards to follow, and some kind of incentive.

Within all structured organisations there also exist informal, non-structured groups. An informal group is created by the members of the group. It consists of two or more people, who usually work together, often in close proximity. In contrast to formal group, an informal group selects its own leader, develops its own rules, sets its own performance or behavioural standards, and establishes peer sanctions and rewards. Two types of informal groups can be identified: One type is based on attraction of friendship among its members. Thus, people who often meet after work for talk and games are an informal group. The second type is base on work relationships. It is composed of people who are required to work closely together because of the organisation's structure, although the members may represent various functional activities, for example, in an advertising agency employee representing the media selection, television, radio, and art departments may meet frequently but unofficially. Developing better cooperation is a key reason for this type of informal group. Among people in an informal group there typically exist two elements: mutual trust and mutual interests. Members of an informal group have confidence in other members' ability to keep the information secret. The second element, mutual interest, results because members of an informal group belong to the same organisation.

CENTRALISATION VERSUS DECENTRALISATION

The term centralisation and decentralisation refers to philosophy of organisation and management that focuses on either the selective concentration (centralisation) or the dispersal (decentralisation) of authority within an organisation structure. The question of where authority resides is resolved in an operating philosophy of management – either to concentrate authority for decision-making in the hands of one or a few or to force it down the organisational structure into the hands of many.

Centralisation and decentralisation is relative concept when applied to organisations. The top-level management may decide to centralise all decision-making: purchasing, and staffing operations. Or may it decide to set limits on what can be purchased at each level by Birr amounts, decentralise the hiring decisions to first-level management for clerical workers (retaining authority for managerial decisions), and let operational decisions be made where appropriate.

Some Guidelines: There are guidelines to follow in determining the degree of decentralisation in an organisation.

1. The greater the number of decisions made at the lower levels of management, the more the organisation is decentralised.
2. The more important the decisions made at lower levels, the greater the decentralisation.
3. The more flexible the interpretation of the organisation policy at lower levels, the greater the degree of decentralisation.
4. The more widely dispersed the operations of the organisation geographically, the greater the degree of decentralisation.

The less a subordinate has to refer to his/her manager to a decision, the greater the degree of decentralisation.

DEPARTMENTALISATION

Departmentalisation, or arrangement of work of an enterprise into manageable parts, is an important part of organising. Some words that are synonymous to the word 'department' include 'division', 'branch', 'bureau', 'board' 'subdepartment' and 'squadron'. Departmentalisation involves three steps:

- *Step 1:* Reasonably like or similar tasks are grouped together. For example, production and engineering in another and finance and accounting in a third department.
- *Step 2:* Authority to perform these activities is assigned to a department head, who may be given one of many titles, such as chief, vice-president, chairperson, manager, commander, or administrator.
- *Step 3:* the department head accepts responsibility for achieving organisational goals and is held accountable to a superior for performance.

Major Bases for Departmentalisation (Approaches to Organising)

Whatever the organisation's approaches to its structural design, it should represent the most effective and efficient use for all resources. Each design has its relative advantages and disadvantages. Remember, what works best for one kind of business may not be appropriate for another.

Departmentalisation by Function (The Functional Approach)

Probably the most common approach to organising is the functional approach. It groups activities under the major headings that nearly every business has in common-finance, production, marketing, and personnel. These are the functions of the business, and the entire organisation would be divided into these major areas. It is a view of just how these major functional areas could be organised. Each of the four major functions is broken down into its various subdivisions. (Note the absence of titles. At this point we are not concerned with titles, only the organisational concept.)

The functional approach is a logical way to organise for most businesses. What each person or unit does or will do becomes the basis of organising. This method helps avoid overlap in the execution of basic business activities. Lines are clearly drawn between the functional areas. This organisation simplifies training because it provides for occupational specialization. Production on marketing, for example, can concentrate on training people in their specialty areas.

Difficulties can arise with type of organisational format. Because personnel are separated from one another, their understanding and concern for the specialty areas outside their own are not easy to achieve. This narrowness of viewpoint can lead to communication difficulties and lack cooperation between the functional areas, which can escalate to hostility; there could be a "production position" and a "marketing position" as a normal situation on organisational questions.

Organisation Chart for an Organisation by Function

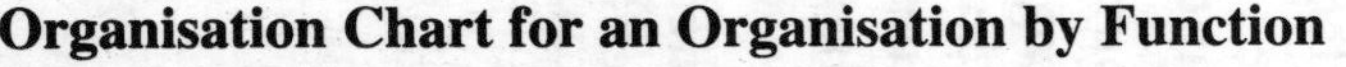

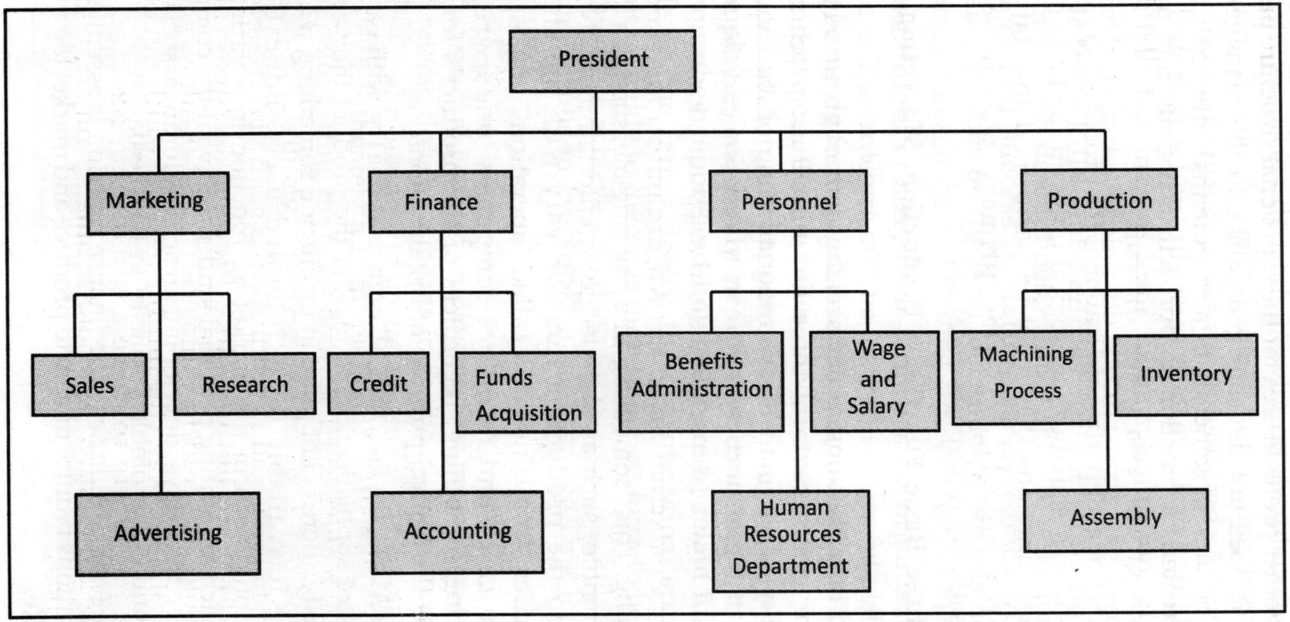

Source: Plunkett, Warren R., and Attner, Raymond F., Introduction to Management; USA Kent Publishing Co. Boston, 1989 p. 197, USA.

Another problem area for the functional structure pattern is that it does not develop generalists in the management area. The lack of generalism and potential internal rivalry that threatens a functional approach to organisation makes economic growth as a system difficult.

Functional departmentalization is the process of grouping organisation's activities into logical units on the basis of the essential functions that must be performed to attain the enterprise's goals. It is the primary way in which organisations are departmentalised.

The Three Basic Functions: Production, Marketing, and Finance

All organisations, profit seeking or non-profit seeking, large or small, perform three key functions: production, marketing, and finance. An understanding of the inherent nature of these functions helps us to comprehend the what, why, and how of departmentalisation by function.

The Production Function: All organisations produce something. This "something" may be tangible, such as a dress, or intangible, such as knowledge or entertainment. Names given to the production function vary with the kind of enterprises. In airlines it is called 'operation', in hospitals 'patient care', and insurance companies 'underwriting'. Producing something, regardless of the product's form or name, is the central purpose of organisations.

The Marketing Function: All organisations try, with varying degrees of sophistication, to market the product they create. Obviously, there is not point in producing something without making it available to its intended users. Educational institutions perform the marketing function in a variety of ways, such as inviting potential students to visit the compass, conduct career days, developing an active alumni association, and obtaining favorable publicity in the media.

The Finance Function: The finance function is essential; all organisations require money to produce and market the utility they offer.

The methods for obtaining capital vary from organisation to organisation. Corporations may sell stocks or borrow money; municipalities tax their residents and may sell bonds; religious and charitable institutions may solicit contributions, and lodge or fraternity may collect dues. Unless there is adequate funding for production and marketing, an organisation cannot achieve its goal. In most businesses the finance department depends on marketing to generate most of the operating capital. However, when additional working or short-term capital is needed the finance function is generally responsible for providing financial base to operate the enterprise, usually through borrowing money or in some instances selling stock.

Departmentalisation by Geographic Area/The Geographic Approach

Geographic departmentalisation is the process of grouping activities by area or territory and assigning them to a given manager. A bank with branches located in various parts of a metropolitan area is departmentalised on a geographic basis, as is an automobile manufacturer that has production facilities located in different areas.

As an organisation grows, larger geographic departmentalisation often becomes necessary. It is virtually inescapable for growing government, business, communication, and military organisations.

With geographic departmentalisation, ultimate authority for performing the three basic organisational functions – production, marketing, and finance is still retained by headquarters. But some authority for their performance is delegated to departments organised on a geographic basis.

Departmentalisation by Customer

Customer departmentalisation is the process of grouping activities in order to serve the needs of specific market segments. Organisation around group of customers makes economic sense when the customers are distinct enough in their demands, preferences, and needs to justify it.

Geographic Organisation Structure

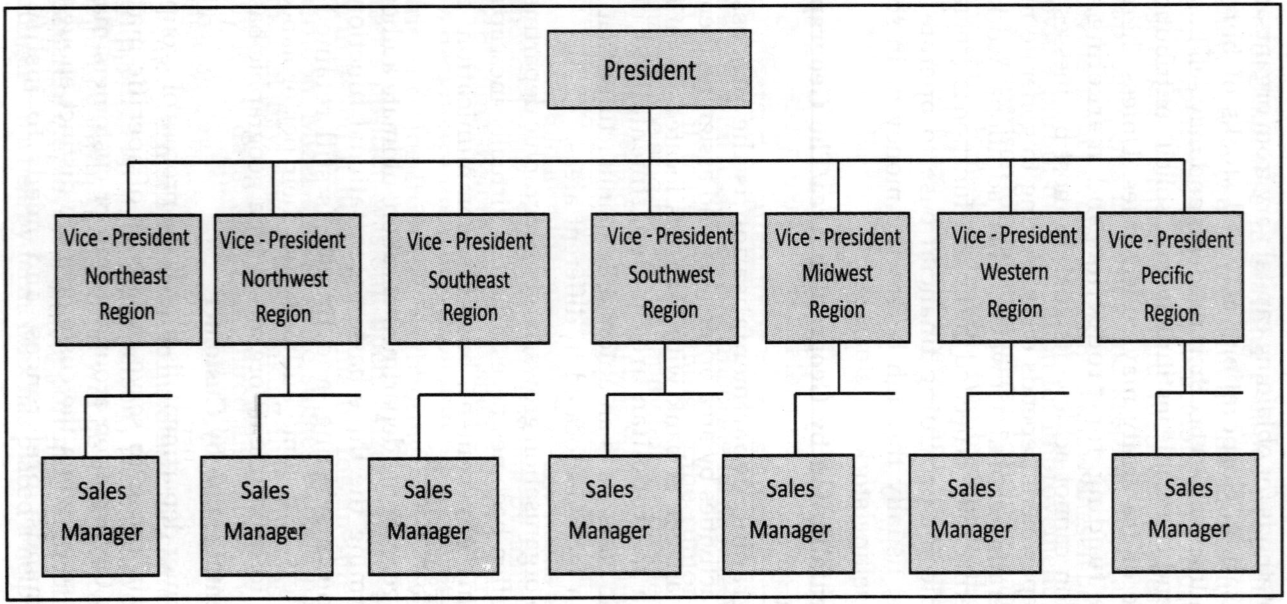

Sales Mgr. = Sales Manager

Source: Plunkett, Warren R., and Attner, Raymond F., Introduction to Management; USA Kent Publishing Co. Boston, 1989 p. 200, USA.

Governments usually demand specialized treatment through their specifications, supervision of production requirements, competitive bidding practices, regulations on employment, and so on. A firm that seeks government contracts often has to have a separate department of specialists who do nothing more than try to interpret and apply various rules, regulations, and procedures that must be compiled with in doing business with a government agency. Chart illustrates a simplified type of functional and customer departmentalisation.

In this context, 'customer' refers to anyone who patronizes an organisation. Synonyms for 'customers' include, depending on type of enterprise, 'clientele', 'patients', 'students', 'enrollees', and similar terms.

Customer departmentalisation is common when an organisation serves people or businesses that have significantly different needs. This form of departmentalisation is undertaken when managers conclude that:

1. Service to customers would be improved and customers loyalty to the organisation would be strengthened; or
2. Greater efficiency would be achieved in the use of personnel, money, and other resources.

Just how far an organisation should carry its customer approach depends on its internal decisions about how best to serve itself and its customers, patients, or clients. It may use this approach for some but not all clients. Customers may be grouped as government, and others, or as a wholesale and retail.

Departmentalisation by Product

The establishment of an organisation pattern based on product should be considered when attention, energy, and efforts need to be focused on an organisation's particular products. This can be true if product requires a unique strategy or production process or distribution system or capital sources. Or it could result if top management tries to focus the energy and the talents of individuals on areas of expertise.

Organisation Chart for an Organisation Organised by Customer

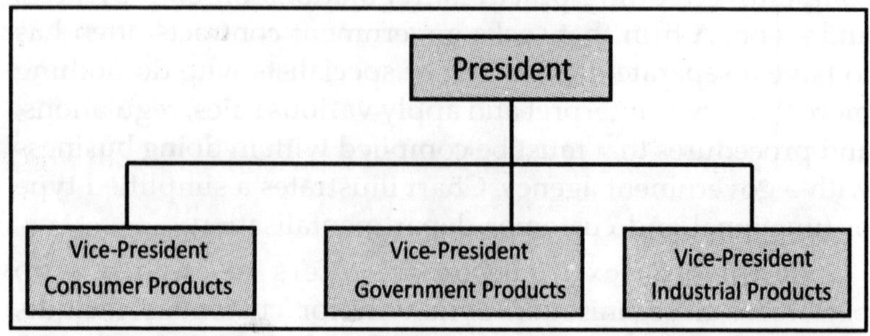

Source: Plunkett, Warren R., and Attner, Raymond F., Introduction to Management; USA Kent Publishing Co. Boston, 1989 p. 203, USA.

With departmentalisation on the basis of products, activities and personnel are grouped according to products or product lines. The major disadvantage is similar to that of the geographic structure – cost through duplication of business functions within each product line. Each needs marketing, finance, personnel, and production operations, which may be so specialized they are unable to serve more than product line or division.

Matrix Organisation

The identifying feature of a matrix organisation is that some managers report to two bosses rather than to the traditional single boss; there is a dual rather than single chain of command. The matrix approach utilises the technical resources of an organisation by efficiently allocating the expertise where and when it is needed. It should produce a coordinated effort because it focuses the functional expertise on a project, thus minimising conflict between specialty areas. Every matrix contains three unique and critical roles: The top manager who heads and balances the dual chains of command, the matrix bosses (functional, product or area) who share subordinates, and the managers who report to two different matrix bosses. Each of these roles has its special requirements.

Organisation Chart Illustrating Product Line Organisation (General Motors Corporations)

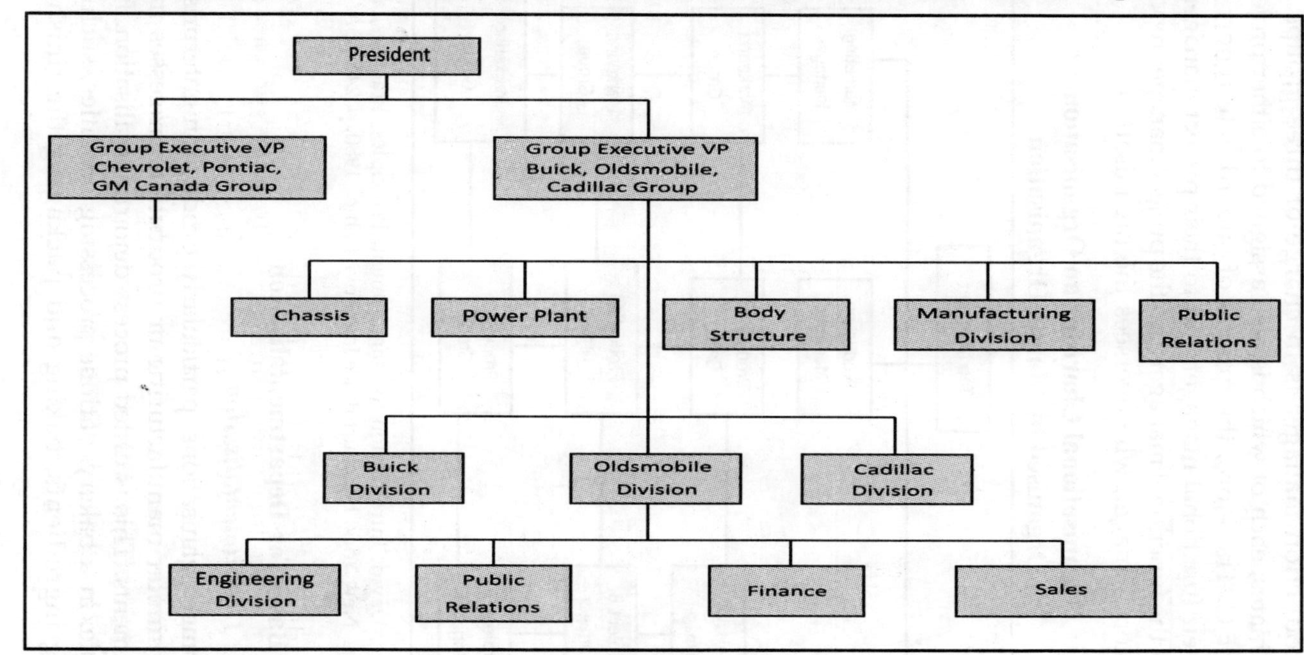

Source: Plunkett, Warren R., and Attner, Raymond F., Introduction to Management; USA Kent Publishing Co. Boston, 1989 p. 202, USA.

The production manager is in charge of three groups of subordinates, each of which is also assigned to either project A, B, or C. Therefore, the groups of subordinate report to both their functional manager and to their project managers. In turn, the functional manager and the project manager report to the top manager, who oversees the organisation.

Organisational Chart for an Organisation Organised by Matrix Organisation

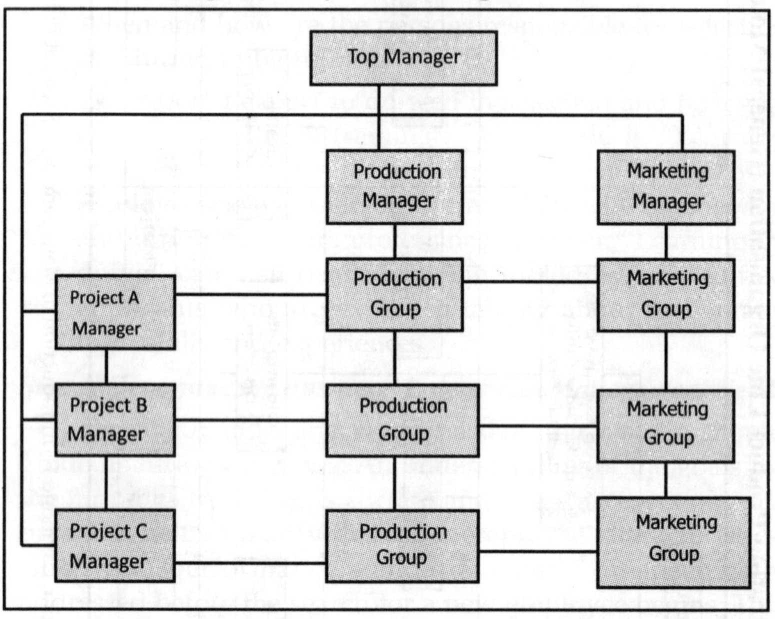

Schwartz, David, Introduction to Management: Principles, Practices, and Processes, New York: Harcourt Brace Jovanovich, Inc., 1980, p. 245 USA.

Other Bases for Departmentalisation

Process Departmentalisation

Some organisations, particularly production enterprises group similar manufacturing or production processes into departments. This is called process departmentalisation. For example, in a bakery, various processing activities, such as mixing ingredients, baking and packaging the finished products, become operating units. Each unit performs as specialised function, and materials, equipment and personnel are assigned to carry it out.

Project Organisation

Project organisation is also often used in professional accounting firms, in which, for example, and accounting specialists may work on a number of different accounts that are under the management of different executives. The project form also has wide application in legal, engineering, consulting, and other enterprises that require the services of highly skilled and specialized personnel.

Taskforce Departmentalisation

A taskforce is a temporary kind of organisation that is formed to study and solve or prepare a recommendation for unique problem that will not likely recur. It typically represents an interdisciplinary approach to goal achievement. A taskforce is used when no one manager has the expertise to solve a problem. Members of a taskforce function as a team. They are selected for their particular expertise as it relates to the problem at hand. For example, senior management in an organisation that has a plan that is not operating efficiently may appoint an interdisciplinary team of experts representing quality control, engineering, production layout, and so on to solve the problem.

Multiple Bases for Departmentalisation

Most small organisations are departmentalised only on a functional basis. Medium sized and large organisations may also be departmentalised on the other basis that have been discusses. It is common for an enterprise to maintain separate production departments for various product lines, to maintain special departments based on different categories of customers. A department store chain that operates several branches is departmentalised on the basis of both product line and geography. The chain may also departmentalize on a customer basis, if it opens a division to sell to commercial and industrial buyers.

AUTHORITY: THE CONCEPT AND APPLICATION

Nature, Sources, and Importance of Authority: All managers in an organisation have authority. They have different degrees of authority based on the level of management they occupy in the organisation structure. Authority is a tool of a manager. It can be described as the right to commit resources (i.e. to make decisions that commit an organisation's resources), or the legal (legitimate) right to give orders (to tell someone to do or not to do something). Authority is 'glue' that holds the organisation together. It provides the means of command. How does a manager acquire authority?

It has been said, "authority comes with territory". This means that authority rested in a manager because of the position he/she occupies in the organisation. Thus, authority is defined in each manager's job description or job charter. The person who occupies the position has its formal authority as long as he/she remains in the position. As the job changes in scope and complexity so should the amount and kind of formal authority possessed.

Even though a manager has formal or legitimate authority it is wise to remember that the willingness of employees to accept the legitimate authority is a key to effective management. The acceptance theory of authority focuses on the employee as the key to the manager's use of authority. In actuality, it is the interaction of formal authority and employee acceptance that provides for positive experience. It is possible for two managers to occupy identical position of formal authority, with the same degree of acceptance of this authority by their employees, and still not to be identically effective in the organisation. Why? One manager may not possess the power to be as effective as another manager.

The Importance of Delegation

Delegation of authority, or the power to act, is inherent in the organising process. Delegation is a concept describing the passing of formal authority to another person. Superiors delegate, or pass authority down, to subordinates in order to facilitate work being accomplished. Delegation may become necessary when managers are absent from their jobs or just may be the philosophy of the manager in order to develop subordinates.

Failure to delegate can create many problems. Overworked managers, lack of time to handle important matters, mistakes, and other forms of inefficiency can result when work is not delegated skillfully. Without delegation no organisation can function effectively.

In general, the more authority delegated to lower-level employees, the more decentralized the organisation is said to be. Conversely, the more authority retained by higher-level managers, the more centralized the organisation is said to be.

Advantages of Delegation

1. Delegation is essential to obtain prompt action.
2. Delegation enables managers to perform higher-level work.
3. Delegation can be a training experience for supportive staff.
4. Delegation can result in better decisions.
5. Delegation can improve morale.
6. Disadvantages of delegation.

SPAN OF MANAGEMENT

Another basic aspect of organising is span of management. Span of management – sometimes called "span of supervision", "span of executive control", or "span of responsibility" – refers to the number of persons one manager can supervise effectively. There is no correct number for the span of control. It is determined for each manager based on the interplay of the complexity and variety of subordinates' work, the ability and training of the subordinates, the ability of the manager, and the organisation's philosophy for centralization or decentralization of decision-making.

Span of management is an important consideration, since it directly affects the efficiency of the organisation. For example, if the span is too wide (that is, an excessive number of people report to one manager), subordinates will receive less supervision than they need and various forms of waste will occur.

As a general rule, the more complex a subordinates' job, the fewer should be that manager's number of subordinates. Another predictable guide is that the more routine the work of subordinates, the greater the number of subordinates that can be effectively directed and controlled. Because of these general rules, organisations always seem to have narrow spans at their tops and wider spans at lower levels. The higher one goes in the organisation's hierarchy, the fewer will be his/her subordinates.

Just how many subordinates should any one manager have? The answer to this question depends on many factors and must be determined with a specific manager or job in mind. How much is the organisation asking this manager to control? How are the tasks to be divided? What resources – people, money, and time – are available? If a manager has too many people to supervise, his/her subordinates will be frustrated by their inability to get immediate assistance from or access to their boss. Time and other resources could be wasted; and plans, decision, and actions might be delayed or made without proper controls or safeguards. On the other hand, if a manager has too few people to supervise, his/her subordinates either overworked or over-supervised and could become frustrated and dissatisfied.

Managers having the same job may not be able to do so. Why? Because no two managers are equal and their subordinates will have differing capabilities and levels of experience as well. The qualifications of the managers and their subordinates must be considered when creating spans of control. The more capable and experienced the subordinates, the more that can be effectively supervised by one competent manager; the less time needed to train and train and acclimate, the more there is to devote to producing output. In general, plans can be widened with the growth in experience and competence of personnel – thus, the continuing need for training and development.

Another factor that can influence the span of control of a manager is the organisation's philosophy toward centralization in decision-making. What is this issue of centralization? We will examine the concept and then relate it to the span of control in this chapter later.

Span of Management and the Exception Principle

According to this principle a manager should handle only exceptions to previously stated rules, procedures, and policies; routine decision should be handled by subordinates. In other words, all work in an organisation should be performed at the lowest competent level. For example, under an existing rule, employees at an airline ticket counter accept all credit cards that are current and not on the list of delinquent customers. A supervisor becomes involved only when an exception occurs – when the card is not current or is listed as delinquent.

If the exception principle is applied properly, managers need not become involved in routine decisions and thus have more time available to plan, train employees, and so on. The net result is that a manager can supervise more people, the span of supervision is wider, and management costs are reduced.

Unfortunately, the exception principle is often overlooked. Violation of exception principle can lead to negative consequences. This may lead to employ managers, and as a result operating costs may unnecessarily become high. Overall operational performance may be reduced because senior level people neglect more important duties. Lower level people are not assigned to work, may miss an opportunity to improve their job skills.

Staffing

MEANING AND DEFINITION OF STAFFING

Koontz & O'Donnel – The managerial function of staffing involves managing the organisation structure through proper and effective selection, appraisal and development of personnel to fill the roles designed into the structure.

Theo Hainmann – Staffing function is concerned with the placement, growth and development of members of the organisation whose function is to get things done through the efforts of other individuals.

STAFFING PROCESS

The staffing function can be viewed as consisting of a series of steps that managers perform to provide the organisation with the right people in the right positions. The following are the eight steps in the staffing process.

1. *Human resource planning:* The purpose of human resource planning is to ensure that the personnel needs of the organisation will be met. An analysis of the plans of the organisation will determine what skills will be needed. Then management can review the present inventory of skills of the organisation and develop a plan to provide the quantity and quality of personnel needed in the future.
2. *Recruitment:* After the human resource needs are determined, managers undertake recruitment to locate

prospective employees. They may accomplish it through newspaper and professional journal advertisements, employment agencies, contacts at trade schools or colleges, and internal sources of the organisation.

3. *Selection:* The selection process involves evaluating the candidates and choosing the one whose credentials match job requirements. The steps in the selection process may include completing and application blank, interviews, reference check, and physical examination.
4. *Induction and orientation:* This step integrates the selected employee into the organisation. Processes include organisational socialization with the work group and becoming acquainted with the organisation's policies and rules.
5. *Training and development:* Both training and development are concerned with improving the employee's ability to contribute to organisational effectiveness. Training involves the improvement of employee skill. Development concerns the preparation of the employee for additional responsibility or advancement.
6. *Performance appraisal:* This step is one of appraising the employee's performance in relation to job standards and then providing feedback to the employee.
7. *Employment decisions: rewards, transfers, promotions, demotions*. The appraisal of performance results in management's making employment decisions, areas of which are monetary rewards, transfers, promotions, and demotions.
8. *Separations:* The dynamics of the staffing process involve both inflow and outflow of people. Managers are concerned with voluntary turnover, retirements, layoffs, and terminations.

Staffing Function

Management teams on successful farms excel at many human resource management skills. Staffing (including recruiting, selecting, hiring and training of employees) is among the skills that become more important as the complexity and overall level of performance of a farm business increases. With increasing size and improving performance comes people complexity: more things accomplished through employees, more delegation to key employees and more reliance on employees to maintain a routine that assures superiority. Any cynical attitudes managers have about employees need to be replaced with positive attitudes.

The organising function of management defines each position or category of positions on the farm. Staffing follows with the filling and keeping filled all positions on the farm. Recruiting a pool of applicants for a position, selecting new employees from among the pool of applicants, training new employees and retraining experienced employees are the key elements of the staffing function. Managing resignations and discharges is also part of staffing. Staffing may be mistakenly limited to regular employees. Instead, staffing includes all personnel categories: managers, working managers and labourers; family and non-family; paid and unpaid; and full-time and part-time.

Practically all farms function without a personnel department. This means that management generalists rather than personnel specialists handle staffing. The farm human resource managers must deal with factors external to the farm such as labour laws and regulations, labour markets, practices of other employers and stereotypes of farm employment. Internal factors such as policies regarding family members entry into the business, conflict between family and business goals and limited opportunities for promotion because of flat organisation charts must be dealt with. Staffing has both short-run and long-run ramifications. In the short-run, positions must be kept filled with qualified people who can get the work done. In the long run, development of top and middle level management personnel for business continuity into the next generation tops the list of staffing challenges.

Staffing success depends heavily on the planning and organising functions of management. In planning, both farm goals and employees' goals are considered. A business functions best when business and employee goals are compatible. Job analysis leads to job specifications and job descriptions. In developing job specifications, the necessary knowledge, skills and abilities for each position are determined. Job descriptions identify specific tasks for each position. Full success in staffing rarely comes without analysing the jobs on the farm, determining what is needed for success in each job and writing a description of the job.

Regardless of size, each farm has an organisational structure. The structure may be the result of careful planning. It may be highly formal with an organisation chart well known and understood. On the other hand, structure may be the result of tradition and happenstance. In may be so informal that employees and family members are unsure of their roles, to whom they report and how they are to relate to other people on the farm. Ideally, the organisational structure provides a guide to the roles that people perform to help the farm business achieve its goals. An effective organisational structure results in everyone on the farm working together as a team.

Work is directed to accomplishing both the farm's goals and the personal goals of employees. Organising must result in tasks being done as a means to an end rather than an end. Structuring the business to create a positive environment for people and ultimately a high quality of work life is equally important to getting the tasks done. Staffing is best done with attention to recruiting, selecting and training employees to help them satisfy their goals and the goals of the business.

The following assumptions provide the context for our discussion of staffing:

1. The mission for the farm has been given careful attention by top management and distributed to the management team and all employees, i.e., the reasons the farm is in business are known.

2. A management team is in place and able to divide up responsibilities. Top management is willing and able as needed to delegate responsibilities and authority.
3. Key positions, e.g., a herdsperson, head milker, full-time crops and machinery person, or a full-time office person are being filled. The process for filling key positions can be modified for part-time and temporary positions.
4. The person hired will be trained to carry out the responsibilities of the position, i.e., it is not necessary to hire a person who already knows how to do the job.
5. No selection process can guarantee selection success. Even if the 'right' person was hired based on all the information available to the employer at the time the decision was made, six months, a year or three years later, it may seem that the 'wrong' person was hired.

Staffing Success — More than Luck

Staffing success is having the 'right person' in a position, rather than simply filling a position. Too often there is an assumption that luck is a key element in staffing. Consequently, a labour manager may place too little emphasis on what can be accomplished through improved recruitment, interviewing, selection and training. The following comment by an agricultural employer illustrates this point:

> "We spent more than one week selecting a truck and body. We spent almost no time at all selecting or training a driver for this truck even though the driver's wages are the largest single cost of operating the truck. In addition, the driver could cause an accident resulting in a financial loss many times greater than the cost of the truck".

Hiring a full-time farm employee or a key part-time employee should be considered a major decision, ranking in importance with decisions on purchase of machinery and land, and construction of facilities. This suggests that a farm manager should carefully plan a staffing strategy following some specific guidelines rather than simply "hoping for the best."

Starting with a Self-Assessment

The following guidelines can help a farm manager evaluate his or her recent staffing efforts and improve in the future:

1. Know yourself;
2. Know your business; and
3. Know the strengths and weaknesses of farm employment.

Know Yourself

Knowing oneself can be an important self-improvement aid. Self-analysis is difficult and fraught with error. No simple written tests exist to provide easy improvement in staffing effectiveness. Nevertheless, an honest agree or disagree reaction to each of the following ten statements should provide some assistance in self-analysis:

1. I am the kind of person I would like as a 'boss'.
2. I don't like to be thought of as the 'boss'.
3. I am highly respected by the people I supervise.
4. I enjoy conversation.
5. I am a good teacher.
6. I am a good listener.
7. I have little trouble being understood by others.
8. I trust the people I supervise.
9. I believe most of the people I supervise like having some responsibility.
10. I believe farm workers regularly need a pat on the back.

The first three statements are concerned with self-image. Statements four through seven focus on communication. The last three statements are concerned with a labour manager's attitude toward employees. Statements with which a labour manager disagrees may suggest areas for improvement. Analysing and altering the personal characteristics associated with each of the statements could be helpful. Understanding his or her strengths and weaknesses can change what the labour manager considers desirable and undesirable characteristics of employees.

Total success in staffing escapes even those labour managers who can 'agree' with all ten statements. The best 'people' persons, best communicators, and those with the most positive attitudes toward their employees still have disappointments in getting and keeping their farms staffed with the 'right people'. Working to know oneself better simply provides part of the foundation for improvement in staffing.

Comparison to other managers also helps a manager better understand himself or herself. Two hypothetical employers, Mizer and Max, provide a standard for employer self-evaluation.

Mizer - Farmer Mizer wants to minimise the time spent in filling a position. The position is vacant because an employee resigned unexpectedly and left the next day. Mizer heard that Joe, a person reputed to be an outstanding employee, is unhappy with his job on a neighboring farm. Mizer called Joe and asked if there was anything to the rumor that he is unhappy. Joe said he was unhappy but the problem has been resolved. Mizer replied that that was too bad because he would have offered him a good job. The same day, one of Mizer's employees told him that his brother-in-law needs a job. Mizer responded with enthusiasm, "Bring him by tonight so I can talk to him." Before Mizer finished eating lunch that same day, the phone rang. The person introduced himself as Kevin, a friend of Joe from the neighboring farm. Kevin asked if Mizer's position was still open. Mizer replied that it was. Kevin asked if he could come by for an interview that afternoon. Mizer smiled as he suggested 2:00 p.m. By 3:00 p.m. that day, Mizer was thinking that this was one of his truly lucky days. Kevin was hired and started working the following day.

Max - Farmer Max wants to maximize the chances of filling each position with the 'right person'. He will have a position open in 30 days. The position will be vacant because one of the current employees has an opportunity to become 'orchard manager' on a nearby farm. Max has placed a help wanted ad in two newspapers. He has heard that Joe, an outstanding employee working on a neighboring farm is unhappy. He called Joe and asked if he was interested in submitting an application for the position. Max also talked to his four employees about the upcoming opening and encouraged them to think about people who might be interested in applying. Within three weeks, Max had 12 applicants. Based on applications and references, he selected seven to be invited for interviews. Four were no longer interested in the position. Three were interviewed. The two most promising were invited back for a second interview that included the other four employees. After extensive discussion with the people who had done the interviewing. Max selected a person who is working in a small factory nearby. The new employee will not start for two weeks. He wants to be fair to his current employer by giving her two weeks notice of his leaving. Max and his four employees look forward to having an outstanding person join them to learn the new job.

Know your Business

An understanding of the goals for the farm business and its current and long run constraints to progress will help in identifying desirable characteristics for employees. Goals and performance standards for the enterprises with which the employee will have direct contact should be specifically addressed before the search for a new employee is started or a training programme implemented. This helps identify those specific things expected to be accomplished through hired farm employees in general and new employees in particular. For example, if an objective is to decrease machinery repair costs, one alternative is to look for a person who has excellent mechanical skills from a previous position. An alternative is to hire an inexperienced person who has a willingness and desire to master the needed mechanical skills. A follow up training programme for such a person can result in a high quality employee.

Clearly, the farm management team has the responsibility for addressing the farm's key problems. These responsibilities cannot be delegated to labour. However, a farm can benefit a great deal from emphasizing complementarity of knowledge, skills and abilities in the labour force rather than settling for duplication and competition.

Know the Advantages and Disadvantages of Farm Employment

Farm employment has advantages and disadvantages. No one position has all the advantages or disadvantages. Positions on some farms may have few of the typical disadvantages. Nevertheless, the farm manager is likely to encounter the following kinds of preconceived notions about the disadvantages of farm employees as positions are discussed with potential and current employees.

Typical advantages of farm employment are:

1. Work with plants and modern machinery.
2. Work varies during the year.
3. Both indoor and outdoor work are included.
4. Sense of accomplishment through observing the farm's progress.
5. Little chance of unemployment.
6. Little or no time spent commuting to work.
7. Easy to find a different farm job.

Typical disadvantages are:

1. Low income relative to non-farm employment.
2. Length of work day and work week.
3. Different benefits than non-farm workers receive.
4. Greater likelihood of injurious accidents.
5. Difficult to advance without changing jobs.
6. Low prestige.
7. Social isolation.

Good labour management involves trying to overcome as many of the disadvantages of farm employment as is feasible while capitalizing on the advantages. For example, one may be able to rotate work schedules so that all employees have at least one day off each week. One may also be able to offer an employee the choice of higher cash wages and the opportunity to rent a house from the employer rather than making the house and lower cash wages a required part of the compensation package. Job titles, trips out of the county for production and seminars, and employee's names printed on their work shirts increase the prestige of farm employment.

Steps for Filling a Position

Following some proven guidelines increases the chances of finding and keeping desirable employees. However, no process can guarantee selection success. Even if the seemingly "right" person was hired six months, a year or three years ago, now it may seem that the "wrong" person was hired. The following eight-step process increases the chances of hiring success:

1. Determine the business' labour and management needs
2. Develop a current job description
3. Build a pool of applicants
4. Review applications and select those to be interviewed
5. Interview
6. Check references
7. Make a selection
8. Hire

Preliminaries to Implementing the Eight Steps

The process for filling a position varies from farm to farm. Previous experiences, nature of the positions being filled, expertise of the selection team, budget for the selection process and time made available for selection are examples of the kinds of factors that affect the design of the selection process. Top management answering the following questions should result in a workable process:

1. To whom, if anyone, is responsibility and authority for filling positions being delegated?

Top management, e.g., the owner/operator of the farm, may retain responsibility and authority for filling positions. On the other hand, it can be delegated to a herdsperson, an assistant farm manager or some other key management person. Someone must have the explicit responsibility and authority. Everyone being responsible often means the task is treated as if not one were responsible.

2. When and how are the persons responsible for selection and hiring to be trained?

   One can not expect to do well in selection and hiring of employees without training in how to do it. "Learning by doing" can result in many potentially valuable employees being lost to other employers who do selection and hiring in a more professional manner. "Learning by doing" can also result in being fooled by unqualified applicants who are expert in talking about their many farm skills and experiences.

Step 1: Determine the Business' Labour and Management Needs

The labour and management needs of the business should guide its hiring decisions. An understanding of the goals for the farm business and its current and long run constraints to progress helps identify desirable employee characteristics. Goals and performance standards should be specifically addressed before the search for a new employee begins. This helps identify those specific things expected to be accomplished through hired farm workers in general and new employees in particular.

Clearly, the management team has the responsibility for addressing the farm's key problems. These responsibilities cannot be delegated to labour. However, a farm can benefit a great deal from emphasising complementarity of knowledge, skills and abilities in the labour force. It makes little sense to hire new people with unneeded strengths and interests that will cause unproductive competition for favoured tasks.

Step 2: Develop a Current Job Description

Job descriptions help both the employer and employees by answering three questions: What does the jobholder do? How is it done? Under what conditions is it done? The job description has at least four parts:

1. Job title;
2. A brief one or two sentence summary of the job;
3. A detailed listing of the major tasks involved in the job summarised under three to seven general headings; and
4. A listing of the knowledge, skills and abilities necessary to do the job.

Job descriptions are typically one page long. The brevity requires a terse, direct writing style. Simple words with single meanings should be used. Action verbs in the present tense should be used in defining the job duties, e.g., milks twice per day five days per week, completes a performance evaluation at least annually for each employee supervised. The specifics of the job should be clear from the job description. The job title, job summary and description of duties should be completely consistent. To illustrate, the job title of herd manager is inconsistent with a list of job duties that includes only labour tasks such as milking, cleaning, feeding, moving, loading, and repairing.

Managers working closely with employees should update job descriptions at least annually. The important tie between job descriptions, performance evaluation and merit pay increases is lost when job descriptions are hid away in a forgotten file.

Step 3: Build a Pool of Applicants

Although there are many methods of getting job applicants, word of mouth and help wanted ads are likely to generate the most applicants. Word of mouth involves current employees, neighbors, agribusiness contacts, veterinarians and others who come in contact with potential employees. Word of mouth is fast and low cost. However, it limits the scope of the job search because qualified applicants may not hear about the position. Current employees enthusiastic about their jobs can become highly effective recruiters.

Help wanted ads can be placed in newspapers and magazines known to be read by potential employees. Help wanted ads have the potential of expanding the applicant pool beyond the local community. The ads may increase the pool of applicants to the point that screening based on their application forms will be necessary. Only well prepared help wanted ads are likely to be effective. Following a seven-step process should result in an effective want ad:

1. Lead with a positive statement or job characteristic that attracts attention.
2. Give the job title.
3. Say something positive about the farm.
4. Describe the job.
5. Explain qualifications necessary for success in the position.
6. Provide information on wages and benefits, as appropriate.
7. Indicate how to apply for the job.

Each applicant should fill out an application form. Taking time to develop an application form or modify one used previously forces identification of important characteristics to look for in applicants. An application form provides a common base of information about all employees being considered. It also provides an important source of questions to be followed up on during the interview.

Step 4: Review Applications and Select those to Be Interviewed

Some applicants will be excluded from further consideration based on the application form. A pre-interview can also be used to help identify applicants to be invited for a formal interview. Having interested people visit the farm to fill out an application form can provide opportunity for a few general questions about experience and interest in the job.

Promising candidates can be given a mini-tour of the farm providing opportunity for general conversation about the dairy industry, livestock, farm work and machinery. The objective of the pre-selection step is to reduce the applicant pool to the most promising candidates. However, the applicant pool should not be reduced to fewer than three people. You may not be successful in hiring the best person in the pool of applicants. Interviewing may dramatically change the pre-ranking of applicants you have made. Also, some applicants will withdraw. Most important, the person hired should know that he or she is a winner having been selected over other qualified people.

Step 5: Interview

Farm employers use applicant interviews more than any other selection tool in deciding whom to hire. Employers can lose outstanding applicants through poor interviewing. On the other hand, they can use excellent interviewing skills to help sell a job opportunity to applicants.

Use these questions to guide preparation for interviewing:

1. Who will be on the interview team?
2. How will we divide time between the formal interview and informal discussion including a farm tour?
3. What questions will we ask in the interview?
4. How will we record our evaluations of each interviewee?
5. Where will we conduct the interview?

Avoid questions that can be answered yes or no. Some examples are:

- Do you like cows?
- Can you drive a tractor?
- Are you afraid of cows?

Instead of these yes/no type questions, use open-ended questions that encourage applicants to explain experiences, characteristics and ideas in their own words. The open-ended questions should be geared toward the following general areas: previous job accomplishments and achievement; non-job accomplishments and achievements; motivation and ambition; hobbies and use of leisure time; and 'what if'. Some examples are:

- What has been your most important accomplishment in your current position?
- What are you looking for in an ideal job?
- When you are working on a project, how do you know you are doing a good job?
- Outside your work, what has been your most important accomplishment thus far in your life? How could this accomplishment help you help our farm?
- What hobbies and spare time activities do you have that would help you help our farm?
- What is your most important strength that would help our farm?

'What if' questions should also be included. They present the applicant a practical problem situation for solution. An applicant for a herd manager position might be given a 'sick cow' situation, an applicant for a machinery operator position might be given a 'tractor won't start' situation, and an applicant for a position with supervisory responsibilities might be given an "employee not cleaning the equipment" situation.

Do not ask questions about: race, color, religion, national origin, marital status, number and care of dependents, height, weight, education unrelated to the job, friends or relatives who have previously worked on your farm, age, arrest or conviction records, U.S. citizenship, credit ratings, handicaps or disabilities, person to notify in case of emergency, sexual orientation, nonbusiness-related references, social clubs and organisations, and military experience in the armed forces of another country. A general guideline is to ask only about those things that are unquestionably related to the job and any applicant's ability to do the job.

It is possible to get necessary information without asking improper questions. It is legitimate to ask about availability for work on weekends and staying late during planting and harvest seasons. However, these questions should not be asked in terms of family responsibilities, children or religious practice. It is important to know if an applicant is a U.S. citizen or whether the applicant meets immigration law requirements. These questions can be asked without reference to national origin.

The interview can be divided into the following nine steps:

1. Relax the applicant and build rapport. (2-3 minutes)
2. Give the applicant a copy of the job description and describe the job in considerable detail. (3-5 minutes)
3. Determine the accuracy of the information on the application form. (4-7 minutes)
4. Ask a series of open-ended questions previously prepared. (10-15 minutes)
5. Encourage the applicant to ask questions. (2-5 minutes)
6. Summarize your farm's mission, objectives, and business philosophy. (2-4 minutes)
7. Summarize the opportunities provided to the person in the position. (2-4 minutes)
8. Encourage the applicant to ask questions. (2-10 minutes)
9. Close with information about plans for making a decision. (2-4 minutes)

The total time for the interview should range from about thirty minutes to about sixty minutes.

A thorough understanding of each step is important:

1. Relax the applicant and build rapport. (2-3 minutes)

   Although this step should take no more than 2-3 minutes, it is important to all the steps that will follow in the interview. The objective is to set the stage for a friendly and open exchange of information. Your smile and warm welcome are important. Possible discussion topics include the weather, any difficulty in finding the farm, a school attended by both interviewer and interviewee, or a friendly dog who enthusiastically greets all visitors.

Confirming that the applicant has parked in the right place may be helpful. Maintain a casual and non-interview atmosphere during this step.

2. Give the applicant a copy of the job description and describe the job in considerable detail. (3-5 minutes)

   It is essential that the applicant understand the job you are filling. Do not depend on general terms like milker, taking care of calves, driving tractor and general farm work. These terms vary substantially from farm to farm. Be specific about the duties and responsibilities.

3. Determine the accuracy of the information on the application form. (4-7 minutes)

   Review the applicant's training directly required for performance of the job, job experience directly related to the position you are filling, and gaps of time between jobs. Pay particular attention to vague reasons for leaving previous positions.

4. Ask a series of open-ended questions previously prepared. (10-15 minutes)

   Your careful preparation for the interview should be apparent to the applicant. Avoid groping for the next question to ask. Impress the applicant with your ability to ask questions that are fun to answer. Keep reminding yourself that you are conducting an interview not an interrogation.

5. Encourage the applicant to ask questions. (2-5 minutes)

   Note that thus far in the interview, the applicant has been responding. At this point, the applicant is given explicit encouragement to ask questions. You should answer the questions in a straightforward manner. Note carefully the content of the applicant's questions, the insight shown, and the follow up questions when pursuing a particular point. Pay careful attention to hints about the needs the applicant hopes to satisfy through the job.

6. Summarize your farm's mission, objectives, and business philosophy. (2-4 minutes)

   This is a 'selling' step. You want the applicant to have a positive impression of your business even if an offer will not be forthcoming. Take time to explain the uniqueness of your business, the importance of people in accomplishing your goals and your vision of the opportunities in the dairy industry. Also explain the pride you have in former employees who have moved up in the industry.

7. Summarize the opportunities provided to the person in the position. (2-4 minutes)

   You now turn from the general summary about the farm business to a specific summary about the position you are filling. This is also a 'selling' step. It is appropriate to again explain the importance of the position to the success of your business, the opportunities there will be to learn the necessary skills for success, and the satisfaction that can be gained through the position.

8. Encourage the applicant to ask questions. (2-10 minutes)

   This second opportunity for the applicant to ask questions should be used to emphasize your desire to be an open and effective communicator. Show your caring attitude. The applicant may have thought of additional questions or now has the courage to ask questions that earlier seemed too daring. This second opportunity for the applicant to ask questions further encourages the applicant to interview you instead of just being interviewed by you.

9. Close with information about plans for making a decision. (2-4 minutes)

   Be specific about what happens next, when you will complete interviews and when you plan to be back in touch with the applicant. Be sure the applicant does not leave guessing about what the next step is. Be careful not to raise the applicant's expectations. Simply express appreciation for the applicant's time, provide your name and telephone number, and welcome personal contacts should the applicant have any questions.

Interviewing is difficult. Knowing how to do it well makes it enjoyable. Some do's and don'ts can serve as reminders on how to improve your interviewing skills.

Do:

1. Make sure the applicant does most of the talking.
2. Make the interview fun for you and the applicant.
3. Listen!
4. Be attentive.
5. Concentrate on the interview and what the applicant is saying
6. Show enthusiasm throughout the interview.
7. 'Read' nonverbal messages.
8. Show appreciation for the person being interested in the position.
9. Show pride in your business and the dairy industry.
10. Stay in control of the interview.

Don't:

1. Project the answer you want from the applicant, e.g., "You do likes cows don't you".
2. Cut an interview short because the first ten minutes didn't go well.
3. Let your note taking during the interview detract from the 'flow' on the interview.
4. Read questions to the applicant.
5. Let your facial expressions and other nonverbal responses show your dissatisfaction with the applicant's answers.
6. Add a series of follow up questions to explore 'interesting' side issues.
7. Allow an aggressive applicant to ignore your questions and talk about things not on your agenda.

8. Go into the interviews with the intention of simply confirming that a pre-interview favorite is in fact the best candidate for the position.

Immediately after the interview and certainly before interviewing another candidate, you should complete an interview form and summarise your impressions of the applicant. Relying on memory to recall key points about applicants will lead to confusion among the applicants and vagueness about strengths and weaknesses.

The written summary should include job experiences; notable knowledge, skills and abilities; motivation and energy; overall strengths; and overall weaknesses. The summary should conclude with an overall score for the applicant. This summary should be prepared before discussion with the other interviewers.

After completion of all interviews, the interview team should discuss each applicant and come to a consensus evaluation.

Step 6: Check references

References can confirm information gathered through the application form and the interview. References can provide additional information about those applicants to whom you are still giving serious consideration. Some employers skip this step because of previous employers' reluctance to share any useful information out of fear of defamation litigation. Reference checks can still be productive. Personal visits or telephone conversations will be more productive than asking for written comments. Getting references from your personal acquaintances or from people well known in farming circles will be more productive than asking strangers. Asking about the most important contribution the employee has made is likely to be more helpful than asking if the reference knows of any reason you should not hire the person. A reference's tone of voice may express more than the words being said. Asking references provided by the applicant to suggest other people to contact can result in additional useful information.

Keep in mind that some references have reason to give less than candid information. Some employers may praise a problem employee in hope that an offer from another farm will solve a messy problem. On the other hand, some employers may hint at some problems in hopes of preventing you from making an offer to an outstanding employee.

Asking the same carefully prepared questions of each reference will be helpful. Using a structured form can greatly simplify recording information received from references.

Step 7: Make a selection

The objective in making a selection is to be as objective as possible given the job description; knowledge, skills and abilities necessary to do the job and the information available concerning each applicant. Selection biases can easily creep into the selection process. Five potentially important selection biases are:

1. *Stereotyping:* Attributing certain characteristics to a particular group of people. "People who grew up on dairy farms like animals."
2. *Halo effect:* Regarding highly an individual who has characteristics you particularly like. "A person, like me, who drives a Ford, prefers Jerseys and is a Chicago Cubs fan will be a good employee".
3. *First impressions:* Judging prematurely based on appearance, handshake or voice. "He has a good firm handshake, a friendly smile, no ear rings, and short hair. I knew before the interview started that he would be a good employee".
4. *Contrast:* Measuring against the last person interviewed. "After that last person we interviewed, I had begun to think we would never find an acceptable person".
5. *Staleness:* Discounting individuals who were interviewed early in the process by giving preference to the individuals interviewed just before they make the selection.

If no satisfactory applicant is found, start the process over rather than deciding to take a chance on a doubtful applicant. Successful use of this guideline requires that backup labour be available so that they can avoid crisis hiring.

Step 8: Hire a person

Make an oral offer in person or by telephone to your first choice followed by a written offer that summarizes the key conditions of employment. In making the offer, emphasize that the applicant is the first choice among several qualified people. Show enthusiasm and make obvious your hope that this person will soon be joining your farm team.

The written employment agreement can be a letter of explanation or a form with blanks filled in as appropriate. Whatever the form, the agreement should include a description of the job, a statement that the employment is 'at will', compensation, benefits, work schedules and the other important details.

Other applicants interviewed will want to know the outcome of your job search. Every person interviewed should have a follow up message from you. A form letter should be sent to all applicants interviewed saying that the position has been filled and thanking them for their interest in the job. The follow up letter should have a positive tone rather than be a 'I reject you' letter. You can comment on the strong field of candidates, express appreciation for the applicant's interest in the job and perhaps say that his or her application will remain on file in case another position opens up. Such a follow up letter should not give specifics about why another person was selected.

Keeping Employees

Following careful recruitment, selection, hiring, and training, an employee is expected to become an important part of the business. Much has been invested in the employee and much is expected. Taking specific steps to keep the person employed on the farm is likely to be cost effective. Of course, some employees will 'outgrow' their current positions and can advance their careers by changing employers. Nevertheless, excellent labour managers are typically recognised as having low rates of labour turnover. Creating opportunities for employees, effective communication and fair compensation are likely to contribute to the retention of employees.

Creating Opportunities for Employees

Good labour managers are creative. They are regularly challenged to find new ways to keep employees motivated and interested in their work. Creating new opportunities for growth and progress within the farm business is difficult in most situations because of the relatively small number of employees and the lack of variation in job responsibilities within the farm. Therefore, a farm labour manager generally must give special attention to creating opportunities. Among the possibilities are increased involvement in extension meetings and seminars, increased decision making responsibility, partial responsibility for training new employees and supervising other employees, more freedom to work without close or daily supervision, some choice of working hours, and part ownership.

Another aspect of the creative challenge facing a farm employer is development of desirable working conditions. The equipment, machinery, and buildings on the farm directly affect working conditions. Substituting equipment and machinery for labour to make the job physically less demanding may help make a job more attractive. Training programmes to help equip an employee for the job responsibilities also are important to creating desirable working conditions.

Effective Communication

Because labour management involves getting things done through people, the labour manager must communicate with employees. The effectiveness of the communication will directly influence labour management success and labour turnover. A labour manager's communication with employees involves much more than just 'telling them' what they need to know. Furthermore, communication is not limited to verbal exchanges between two or more people. Communication may occur through writing, pictures, charts, and posters. Communication may also be nonverbal, i.e., not involving verbal or written actions. A smile, frown, handshake, shrug, grunt, nod, gesture and even silence are also means of communication.

Not all communication is effective. Effective communication involves being understood and getting desired results. Part of a labour manager's communication success involves being sensitive to communication barriers. This sensitivity includes using words employees understand, being a good listener, encouraging them to ask questions, and avoiding harsh criticism of those who do not understand.

Fair Compensation

Worker compensation or payment may be divided into two parts: dollars and benefits. Farm workers are generally paid less than non-farm workers with comparable skills and job responsibilities. However, the problems associated with compensation are not limited to increasing dollar incomes of workers. In fact, employers who depend solely on pay increases to keep key employees are likely to be disappointed with the results. Clearly, workers' incomes need to be analyzed in terms of what they could earn in other farm and non-farm positions. However, more than the dollar amounts need to be considered in these evaluations. An employee is likely to be particularly sensitive to the benefits received in the farm job compared with the benefits received in non-farm jobs. Examples of such benefits are paid vacation, sick leave, overtime pay, and life and health insurance.

It is important to view benefits from both the employee standpoint and the employer standpoint. For example, a farm employer providing a house to an employee may view the benefit as a way of getting some return from a house that could not otherwise be rented. However, an employee may view the benefit as a negative characteristic of the job because of the employee's family living in an undesirable house or living too close to the 'job'.

Employers often consider wage incentive plans attractive because they tie a worker's earnings to how well a job is done. An assured reward for an employee's high quality performance is seen as a way of reducing labour turnover. However, these wage incentive plans are not a cure all for labour turnover and other labour management problems. Wage incentive plans cannot replace effective recruiting and training of workers. But a wage incentive plan may help keep an outstanding employee. Employers can expect an increased level of productivity and a decreased rate of employee turnover if an employee feels rewarded for efforts to improve production levels. If a worker is dissatisfied by factors other than the rate of pay or working conditions, a wage incentive plan will not reduce labour problems.

If an employer and employee should agree that a wage incentive plan would be desirable, the following steps may be helpful in developing and starting the plan:

1. Specify what is expected to be accomplished with the plan.
2. Identify the employee's concerns, aspirations and abilities.
3. Develop a specific plan.
4. Start the plan.
5. Evaluate the plan.

Training of Employees

No matter how carefully a farm employer recruits and selects employees, they will lack some necessary knowledge and skills. Training is essential if employees are to reach their potential. Training should help them feel like they are creating better opportunities for themselves and at the same helping the farm accomplish its goals.

Training is anything an employer does to help employees learn to do their work the way the employer wants them to do it. Training is an investment in people benefiting both the employer and employee. In an ideal employer-employee situation, the investment in teaching allows an employee to do the job better. Doing the job better benefits both the employee and the farm. Trainers (teachers) are challenged to understand what the employees (learners) know from previous training and experience. Trainers need to see the job through the eyes of the employees. Good training makes complicated and complex tasks seem simple. Note how complicated riding a bicycle seems until one knows how. All experienced computer users know there is not an 'any key' on a computer keyboard. Yet many inexperienced users have searched in vain for such a key to be able to follow the direction in the computer manual that says, "Press any key and continue". Finding pneumonia in the dictionary is possible only if one knows that it begins with a 'p' rather than an 'n'.

The importance of training programmes on farms will increase dramatically. Margins of acceptable error will grow smaller and smaller. Equipment will become more complicated. The work will be more complex. People with all the necessary skills and experience for success on a farm cannot be hired. A decreasing percentage of new employees will have been raised on a farm or will have had previous work experience on a farm. In this environment, labour can easily become the weakest link in the plans for success of the business.

Content of Training

Training of farm workers involves four kinds of learning: knowing, doing, combination of what is known or can be done, and combinations of knowing and doing. Learning infers:

1. Knowing something intellectually or conceptually one never knew before, e.g., visitors can carry disease onto a farm.
2. Being able to do something one could not do before, e.g., train a new employee to clean equipment.

3. Combining two knowns into a new understanding of a skill, piece of knowledge, concept, or behaviour, e.g., knowledge about the causes of pneumonia in pigs and knowledge about air movement in closed buildings combined to understand the importance of ventilation.
4. Being able to use or apply a new combination of skills, knowledge, concepts, or behaviours, e.g., combining mechanical skill, attention to detail, knowing what to listen for, and superior hearing to recognise when a belt needs tightening.

All four kinds of learning should be part of a training programme as appropriate. Training must be more than teaching employees how to do things. Helping them understand the importance of the job, the principles behind the job, and how they can use what they already know are important.

Conditions that Facilitate Learning

Each farm should have a plan for training. The plan should include creation of a positive environment for learning. Reinforcing the following assumptions in each trainer and employee helps create an ideal learning situation:

- All employees can learn.
- Learning should be made an active process.
- Learners need and want guidance and direction.
- Learning should be sequential.
- Learners need time to practice.
- Learning should be varied to avoid boredom.
- Learners gain satisfaction from their learning.
- Correct learner behaviour should be reinforced.
- Learning does not occur at a steady rate.

Training Objectives

An employee training programme should have three distinct phases:

1. Orientation;
2. Learning to do the first job;
3. Preparation for future tasks and responsibilities.

Orientation

A farm employer has only one opportunity to make a good first impression on new employees. The first day that a new person is on the job provides many 'teachable moments'. Nearly all employees want to get off to a good start. The good start depends more on orientation than on how much work the person does the first few hours on the job.

Help every new person get off to a good start. Orientation is as important for the part-time high school worker as for the new full-time employee. Even a relative or nearby neighbor known for years will benefit from careful orientation.

Most employers anticipate some obvious questions. "Where should I park?" "What time do you want me here tomorrow?" "What do you want me to do?" Orientation should go beyond answering these first questions. Here is the opportunity to convince each new person that he or she is important to you and to the farm.

Planning the Orientation - Orientation actually starts with the advertisement of the position, the interview, and the job description given the new employee. Being businesslike in the hiring process is important. A written job description and written offer with the conditions of employment help set a positive tone.

After a person is hired and before the first day of work, several questions need to be answered:

1. Who will be in charge of orienting the new person?
2. What will be the content of the orientation?
3. How will the orientation mesh with job training?

One person should be charged with planning and conducting the orientation. Other people, including employees, can be involved even though responsibility is centered in one person. Orientation should lead smoothly to the start of job training.

Content of Orientation - The specific content of the orientation depends on the size and complexity of the farm. Sensitivity to immediate information needs and postponing the nonessential information to the second phase of training are the keys to successful orientation. Where to park the car, what to wear to work, location of the bathroom, names of co-workers and to whom to go with questions are examples of content essential to orientation. Procedures for arranging which week to take vacation are not.

Following is a list of items to be considered in planning the details of the orientation:

Farm Characteristics

- History of the farm
- Mission statement and goals for the farm
- Management team
- Layout of facilities, buildings and land
- Overview of what the farm produces and production processes
- Role of employees

Personnel Policies

- Policies and rules about such things as attendance,
- breaks, scheduling work, use of equipment and tools, and courtesy to other employees
- Probationary period
- Disciplinary practices
- Safety procedures

Employee Benefits

- Pay and paydays
- Vacation
- Sick leave
- Insurance benefits
- Rest breaks
- Retirement programme

Introductions

- To owner/operator
- To supervisor
- To coworkers
- To people who often visit the farm, e.g., close relatives, person who delivers feed, and veterinarian

Job Duties

- Where the work will be done
- Specific tasks
- Safety precautions
- Relationship of the job to other work on the farm

Key Point - Your reaction to these suggestions may be, "It would be nice but.... I don't have time for this stuff because we've got work to do," or "Only big farms need to worry about these things", or "I hire people to work not learn the history of my farm." Key point — An employer will do better with happy, positive and enthusiastic people than with people who are just there to do a job and go home. Well planned and conducted orientation helps people get off to a good start. It increases their chances of being happy with their jobs and positive about the employer and the business.

Learning to do the First Job

Training the employee to handle the first tasks logically follows from the orientation. As with orientation, employees are generally anxious to learn how to do the first job. The tone and level of expectations set in the orientation should be carried into this phase of training. As with orientation, the emphasis should be on what the person is learning, not on how much work is being done. If a good foundation is laid during orientation and early training, the amount of work being done will be a minor consideration.

Preparation for Future Tasks and Responsibilities

Preparation for future tasks and responsibilities is a continuous process based on the employee's skills and aspirations, and changes in the farm. This phase of training should be well planned for each employee. Performance evaluations can stimulate interest in additional training to be ready for future opportunities.

The relative amount of time devoted to orientation, training for the first job and preparation for future responsibilities vary with the type of employee. Temporary workers may receive only orientation and training focused on the seasonal job, e.g., tractor driving during planting season. Long-term key employees may continue to receive training for both immediate and future tasks and responsibilities for as long as the employment lasts.

Principles of Job Instruction

Job instruction can be divided into getting ready to train and training. Trainers on farms are often so experienced in what they are teaching that taking time to prepare for training seems like a waste of time. "I don't have time to prepare" or "I know this job so well I don't need to think about how to teach it" may be foolish attitudes. Muddled and confused instruction increases the time spent on training and causes frustration for both trainer and employee.

Two important questions guide preparation for training.

1. What is the objective of the training? Define specifically what the learners are to know or be able to do at the conclusion of the training. An acceptable level of performance and timetable for the training should be established.
2. What are the principal steps in the task and in what sequence should they be done? Analysing each task can be helpful. Develop tips on how the job can be made easier, done more quickly or done with less frustration for the employee.

Having answered these two questions, the trainer is ready to prepare equipment, materials, learning aids and the work place for the actual training. Looking for equipment or supplies during training leaves the learner suspicious that the teacher is careless or incompetent or both.

The actual instruction can be aided by a five-step teaching method:

1. *Prepare* the learner. Learners are prepared when they are at ease, understand why they need to learn the task, are interested in learning, have the confidence that they can learn and the trainer can teach. The most important part of learner preparation is creating a need to know or desire to learn on the part of the trainee. It helps to show enthusiasm for the task, relate the task to what the learner already knows, help the learner envision being an expert in the task, have the learner explain how the task will relate to success on a farm, add fun and prestige to the task when possible and associate the task with respected co-workers.
2. *Tell* the learner about each step or part of the task.
3. *Show* the learner how to do each step or part of the task. In demonstrating the task, explain each step emphasizing the key points and more difficult steps. Remember the little and seemingly simple parts of the task. Get the learner involved by asking questions about what is being shown.
4. Have the learner do each step of the task while being observed by the trainer and then without the trainer observing. Ask the learner to explain each step as it is performed. If steps or parts of the task are omitted, re-explain the steps and have the learner repeat them.
5. *Review* each step or part of the task with the learner, offering encouragement, constructive criticism and additional pointers on how to do the job. Be frank in the appraisal. Encourage the learner toward self-appraisal.

Getting Started

Improved training for both new and experienced employees offers farm employers a way to increase employee success. Training programmes rarely change quickly and easily. Deciding what can be accomplished through better training is a good starting point. Create a good environment for learning. Prepare before jumping into changes in training. Learn and use a five-step method, Prepare-Tell-Show-Do-Review, to steer both trainers and employees toward greater success.

Performance Appraisal

No employee escapes performance appraisal. As a minimum, each employee receives informal messages from his or her supervisor and co-workers. The messages may be carefully calculated or emotional outbursts, frequent or infrequent, helpful or hurtful, understood or misunderstood, consistent or inconsistent, fair or unfair. They may improve performance or cause additional performance problems. They may motivate an employee or leave the employee discouraged and disgruntled.

Turning performance appraisal into a positive force challenges even the best farm personnel manager. Three steps are necessary:

1. Establish written standards for employee performance.
2. Develop both supervisor and employee understanding of these standards.
3. Regularly inform employees of how they are performing relative to the established standards.

Effective performance appraisal moves beyond informal communication but does not exclude it. Planned and formal performance evaluation interviews complement spontaneous informal employer-employee interaction about performance.

Few farms have formal employee performance programmes. Spontaneous and informal comments about performance are the norm. Too often, employees are left guessing about the quality of their performance or underrate their performance because of the sharing of negative but not positive evaluations.

Performance evaluation is a complex activity. A formal performance evaluation system can be a realistic long-term goal to work toward. In the short-run, farm employers can take helpful steps toward the long-run ideal. The first step is to develop job descriptions for everyone with everyone's help. These job descriptions evolve continuously rather than being done once and for all. Job descriptions have value only if they are current, in writing, and used regularly to clarify job content, the organisational structure of the business and as a basis for evaluation.

In the short-run, the following statements and questions can guide performance evaluation, counseling and planning discussions with each employee:

1. I see the following three things as your most important strengths.
2. I see the following two things for us to work on improving during the next six months.
3. What do you see as your most important strengths?
4. What would you like to learn or work on improving?
5. How should I work on improving?

Intermediate steps could include clear communication of expectations for employees, regular feedback to employees about their performance, providing employees opportunity to respond to their supervisor's comments and additional training for employees based on needs identified through performance appraisal. The notion of catching people doing things right should be an important part of employee evaluation and improving performance appraisal.

Discipline

High quality farm worker performance requires implementation of carefully made tactical plans. Deviations from the plans by employees results in standards not being met and goals not being accomplished. Managers must deal with employees' deviation from rules, procedures and expected behaviours. Employees coming late to work, not following safety procedures when working alone, not properly cleaning equipment in their rush to get home, and using wrong or wrong amounts of medication are examples of unacceptable behaviour that should be addressed rather than ignored. A cautionary note is in order. Employers can easily confuse discipline problems with selection, training and communication problems. This discussion of discipline applies to those cases in which the employee can reasonably be expected to perform or behave according to established standards, norms or rules, i.e., they have been carefully selected, well trained and are regularly evaluated.

A disciplined person exhibits the self-control, dedication and orderly conduct consistent with successful performance of job responsibilities. This discipline may come through self-discipline, co-workers or the supervisor/employer. Self-discipline is best and most likely to come from well selected, trained, and motivated people who regularly have feedback on their performance.

An employee not performing up to the agreed upon standards or not following the understood rules is subject to punishment, i.e., disciplinary action. Punishing or disciplining employees falls among the least pleasant activities in human resource management. In the short-run, doing nothing or ignoring errant actions and behaviour almost always comes easier than taking the needed action. Not disciplining when needed sends confusing messages to the errant employee, other employees and other managers in the farm business. If starting work at 6:30 a.m. rather than 6:00 a.m. draws no reaction from the employer, does this mean the starting time has been changed to 6:30?

Several guidelines help reduce the compounding of discipline problems with problems in disciplining. Both employers and employees need to know the rules and performance expectations. An employee handbook or other form of written statement provided each employee is basic. Rules should be uniformly enforced among all employees. If special rules apply to a certain employee, e.g., use of the pickup truck without asking permission, other employees need to be so informed. Punishment should be based on facts.

All parties should be heard rather than depending on one person only for facts. Action should be taken promptly. "Saving up" a series of minor problems and infractions for a grand explosion is poor disciplinary practice. All discipline other than discharge should have the objective of helping the employee. Permit the employee to maintain self-respect by disciplining the employee's behaviour or act. Do not berate the person.

Keeping punishment consistent with the severity of an offense challenges all labour managers. Being thirty minutes tardy for work the fourth time in two weeks has to be handled differently from being thirty minutes tardy for the first time in two years. Theft of tools has to be handled differently than tardiness for work. Progressive discipline provides a formal structure within which errant employees can be handled. In progressive discipline, the severity of punishment increases in relation to the seriousness of the offense or the number of times an offense is repeated. Typical levels in progressive discipline are: informal talk and counseling, oral warning or reprimand, written warning, disciplinary layoff and discharge.

Both employers and employees usually react negatively to the atmosphere of conflict and parent disciplining child inherent to progressive discipline. High priority placed on selection, training, informal communication and performance appraisal reduces the need for punishment of employees. Treating employees as adults, expecting them to rely on self-assessment for correcting problems and relying on informal counseling rather than formal reprimands provide an atmosphere of positive discipline.

Directing

LEADERSHIP

Leadership involves other people; therefore, where there are leaders, there must be followers. Leadership can arise in any situation where people have combined their efforts to accomplish a task. Thus, leaders may or may not be managers. Management and leadership are not synonymous. We need to understand the difference between them. A manager is a person formally recognised in the organisation's hierarchy. A manager is expected to plan, organise, control, and make effective decisions. They may or may not be effective in influencing their subordinated toward goal accomplishment. Ideally, all managers should be leader, but many are not. A manager may be able to influence or direct organisation member. But because of an inability to perform the other management function, the manager may fail to get individuals or a group to achieve organisational objectives.

Leadership is not an easy term to define precisely. Plunkett, Warren R. and Attner, Raymond F., (1989) define Leadership as the process of influencing a group of individual to set a goal or achieve a goal. It is a process involving the leader, the led (group or individual), and a particular goal or situation. It is behavioural in nature and involves personal interaction. It is correct to state that a good manager is always a good leader, but a good leader is not necessarily a good manager.

Ivancevich, Donnelly and Gibson/1989/define leadership as the ability to influence through communication the activities of others, individually or as a group, toward the accomplishment of worthwhile, meaningful, and challenging goals.

Importance of Leadership

The leadership relationship is not limited to leader behaviour resulting in subordinate behaviour. Leadership is a dynamic process. The leader follower relationship is reciprocal and effective leadership is a two-way process which influences both individual and organisational performance.

Leadership is vitally important at all levels within the company from main board to the shop floor. Leadership is the moral and intellectual ability to visualize and work for what is best for the company and its employees.

The most vital thing the leader does is to create team spirit around him and near him, not in a schoolboy sense but in realistic terms of mature adults.

Good leadership helps to develop teamwork and the integration of individual and group goals. It aids intrinsic motivation by emphasizing the importance of the work that people do.

Leadership Roles

In interacting with employees in the work environment, a manager must play four basic leadership roles: educator, counselor, judge, and spokesperson. We consider the nature and importance of each.

Educator

All managers must perform the leadership role of educator. Managers fulfill this role by teaching employee's job skills as well as acceptable behaviour and organisation values.

Counselor

A second leadership role of a manager is counselor. This role involves listening, giving advice, and preventing and solving employees' problems. In performing this role, managers are fulfilling two expectations of employees:

1. Awareness of and concern for the individual employee.
2. Assistance in solving a problem.

Judge

Playing the leadership role of judge involves appraising subordinates' performance; enforcing policies, procedures, and regulations', settling disputes', and dispensing justice.

Spokesperson

Managers act as spokespersons for subordinates when they relay their suggestions, concerns, and views to higher authorities.

Approaches in Studying Leadership in Organisations

Leadership has been one of the most studied topics in management, yet the conclusions, reached have been contradictory, exaggerated, and controversial. Part of the problem lies in the definitions, measurement, and theory used to study leadership. Due to the complex and variable nature of leadership, there are many ways of analyzing leadership. It is necessary to have some framework in which to consider different approaches to the study of leadership. One way is to examine managerial leadership in terms of.

1. The qualities or trait approach.
2. The functions or group approach.
3. Leadership as a behavioural approach.
4. Styles of leadership.
5. The situational and contingency models.

The three main approaches at the center of the debate surrounding leadership are as follows:

1. *The leader trait approach* - attributes performance difference among employees to the individual characteristics (traits) of leaders.
2. *The leader behaviour approach* - attributes performance differences to the behaviours and style of leaders.

3. *The situational contingency approach* - the leader's behaviour and style in combinations with situational factors are the key reasons for performance differences.

1. The leader traits approach

The trait (qualities approach) assumes that leaders are born and not made. Leadership consists of certain inherited characteristics or personality traits, which distinguish leader from their followers: the so-called 'Great person' theory of leadership. The qualities approach focus attention on the man in the job and not on the job itself. It suggests that attention is given to the selection of leaders rather than to the training for leadership.

Leadership traits are:intelligence, supervisory ability, initiative, self-assurance and individually in the manner in which work was done.

2. The leader behaviour approach

The disappointing result of the search for leadership traits have led to somewhat a different line of thought. Rather than focusing on the characteristics of effective leaders, an alternative is to focus on their behaviour.

This approach draws attention to the kinds of behaviour of people in leadership association. One of the most extensive research studies behavioural categories of leadership was the Ohio state leadership studies undertaken by the Bureau of Business Research at Ohio State University. The focus was on the Effects of leadership style on group performance.

Consideration and Initiating Structure

Results of Ohio state studies indicated two major dimension of leadership behaviour labeled consideration and initiating structure.

Consideration

Reflects the extent to which the leader shows respect and rapport with the group and shows concern, warmth and support and consideration for subordinates.

Initiating Structure

Reflects the extent to which the leader defines and structures group interaction towards the attainment of formal goals and organises group activities.

Four types of leadership behaviour:

(a) Low on consideration and low on structure.

(b) Low on consideration and high on structure.

(c) High on consideration and high on structure.

(d) High on consideration and low on structure.

3. The situational contingency approach

An increasing number of managers are prone to believe that the practice of leadership is too complex to be presented by unique traits or behaviour. Rather, another idea is that effective leadership depends on situation. This approach concentrates on the importance of the situation in the study of leadership. A variety of people with differing personalities and from different backgrounds have emerged as effective leaders in different situations.

The situational approach stresses the situation as a dominant feature in considering the characteristics of effective leadership. As described by Yalokwu, P.O. (1999), what matters in leadership is obeying the laws of situation. In the ideas of depersonalizing of orders and obeying the law of the situation he emphasizes that what matters is to discover the law of the situation and obey it. One person should not give orders to another person but both agree and take their orders from the situation.

Theory X and Theory Y

Theory Y (Exhibit) depicts the second set of assumptions about work and human nature. A managerial philosophy founded on *Theory Y* will prepare a leader to work with people as individuals, to involve people in the process of decision making, to openly encourage people to seek responsibility, and to work with people to achieve their goals.

Exhibit - Theory X

1. The average human being has an inherent dislike of work and will avoid it if he can.
2. Because of this human characteristic about work, most people must be coerced, controlled, directed, and threatened with punishment to get them to put forth adequate effort toward the achievement of organisational objectives.
3. The average human being prefers to be directed, wishes to avoid responsibility, has relatively little ambition, and wants security above all.

Exhibit - Theory Y

1. The expenditure of physical and mental effort in work is as natural as play or rest. The average human being does not inherently dislike work. Depending on controllable conditions, work may be a source of satisfaction (and will be voluntarily performed) or a source of punishment (and will be avoided if possible).
2. External control and the threat of punishment are not the only means for bringing about effort toward organisational objectives. A person will exercise self-direction and self-control in the service of objectives to which he or she is committed.
3. Commitment to objectives is a function of the rewards associated with their achievement.
4. The average human being learns, under proper conditions, not only to accept, but to seek, responsibility.
5. The capacity to exercise a relatively high degree of imagination, ingenuity, and creativity in the solution of organisational problems is widely, not narrowly, distributed in the population.
6. Under the conditions of modern industrial life, the intellectual potentials of the average human being are only partially utilised.

Leadership Styles

It was defined leadership as influencing others to achieve results. The approaches a manager uses to influence others are elements of the manager's style. These elements, though described individually, in actuality are integrated in leadership. Managers' leadership styles are composed of three parts.

1. How Managers choose to motivate;
2. Managers' decision-making styles; and
3. Manager's areas of emphasis (orientation) in the work environment.

1. Positive or Negative Motivation

Leaders influence others toward goal achievement through their approach to motivation. Depending on the style of the manager, the motivation can take the form of rewards or penalties. Positive leadership style deals in praise and recognition, monetary rewards, increase of security, and additional responsibility. At the other end of the continuum, negative leadership emphasizes penalties; loss of the job, suspension, and public reprimands are extremes of negative leadership. Positive leadership styles encourage development of employees through the creation of higher job satisfaction. Negative leadership styles are based on threats and the ability to withhold items of value from an employee.

2. Decision-Making Style

A second element of a manager's leadership style concerns the degree of decision- making authority the manager grants to subordinates. These styles may range from absolute decision making by the manager, with no opportunity for participation by the subordinates, to decision making by the groups with limits defined by the manager. Robert Tannenbaum and Warren H. Schmidt (1973) have presented this range of decision-making styles in the continuum of leadership behaviour shown in Figure 8.1. Any of these styles is an option a manager can choose to use based on the situation. Notice that the degree of involvement of the employee is greater as you move form left to right

The range of styles shown on the continuum can be grouped under three headings:

1. Autocratic;
2. Participative; and
3. Free-rein.

The numbers under each decision making style are explained as follows:

Autocratic	1= Manager makes decision and announces it
	2= Manager sells decision
	3= Manager presents decision and invites questions
Participative	4= Manager presents tentative decision subject to change
	5= Manager presents problem and gets input, makes decision
	6= Manager defines limits, asks group to make decision
	7= Manager and group jointly make decision
Free-Rein	8= Manager permits employee to function within limits set by manager

Leadership Theories

1. Fiedler's Contingency Theory

Plunkett, Warren R. and Attner, Raymond F. (1989) discuss the model that the most appropriate style of leadership for a manager depends on the situation in which a manager works. The contingency model, which he developed, shows that the effectiveness of a leader is determined by the interaction of the manager's orientation (task or employee) with three situational variables: leader – member relationships, task structure, and leader position power. Having already discussed task and employee orientation in the previous section, we are now ready to examine the three variables so that we can understand the model of contingency theory.

Leader – member relations - Refers to the degree to which the leader is or feels accepted by the group. It is measured by the degree of respect, confidence, and trust the subordinates feel toward the superior. This factor is rated on a scale from good to poor. If the relationship is rated as good, the leader should be able to exercise influence over the subordinates easily. On the other hand, if there is friction or distrust (a poor rating), the manager may have to resort to favors to get performance.

Task structure concerns the nature of the subordinate's job or task. It reflects the degree of structure in the job: A structured job would be routine in nature with prescribed processes. An example would be the position of file clerk. An unstructured job would have complexity and variety and room for creativity.

Leader position power describes the organisational power base from which the individual manager operates. To what degree can the leader punish or reward within the organisation? The power can range from strong to weak.

2. Path-Goal Theory

The *path-goal theory* or leadership is concerned with the ways in which a leader can influence a subordinate's motivation, goals, and attempts at achievement. It suggests that a leadership style is effective or ineffective on the basis of how the leader influences the perceptions of:

- Work goals or rewards of subordinates.
- Paths (behaviours) that lead to successful goal or accomplishment

The origin of this theory is in the expectancy theory or motivation will be discussed later in this Chapter. We recall under that theory that an employee's motivations are influenced by the employee's perceptions of:

1. His or her ability to accomplish a specific task;
2. The relationship of the rewards to the accomplishment of the task; and
3. The value of the rewards offered.

The path-goal theory states that the leader can influence these perceptions of the rewards and can clarify what employees have to do to achieve these rewards.

With this foundation in mind, let's examine the components of the path-goal theory: leader behaviour and situational factors. The theory contains two propositions concerning leader behaviour:

1. Leader behaviour is acceptable and satisfying to subordinates to the extent that they view such behaviour as wither an immediate source of satisfaction or an instrument to future satisfaction.
2. Leader behaviour will increase subordinates' efforts if it links satisfaction of their needs to effective performance and supports their efforts to achieve goal performance.

To do this, the theory provides four types of leadership behaviours based on the work needed. These are:

1. *Instrumental behaviour* (task oriented). It involves the planning, monitoring, and task assignment aspect of leadership. Instrumental behaviour can be used to increase an employee's work effort or clarify outcomes.
2. *Supportive behaviour*. It involves the employee-oriented concern for the welfare and needs of subordinates. In addition, it includes creation of a warm, pleasant climate.
3. *Participative behaviour*. It involves using subordinate's ideas in decision making. A subordinate who operates in dependently and who has ability would respond favorably to this approach.
4. *Achievement-oriented behaviour*. This involves both developing a highly challenging climate for an employee and demanding good performance.

These leadership behaviours are based on the situational factors. There are two situational factors that influence leadership behaviour:

1. The personal characteristics of the subordinates include the person's ability, self-confidence, and needs.

2. The environmental pressures and demands with which subordinates must cope to accomplish goals and satisfy personal needs.

MOTIVATION AT WORK

Motivation is derived from Latin word 'movere' meaning 'to move'. The term motivation is at the very heart of the study of work organisations. It is of great concern to both management and workers in the organisation in spite of its importance, not every one appreciates the full meaning of the concept of motivation. Perhaps, the reason for this is because it is difficult to define and apply it in organisations.

Many researchers and writers have defined motivation in different ways such as:

1. Motivation is defined as "a prepotent state that energizes and guides behaviour" and it is rarely measured directly but is inferred from changes in behaviour or even in attitudes.
2. Motivation is defined as "a predisposition to act in a specific goal directed way".
3. Motivation is defined as "an emotion or desire operating on a person's will and causing that person to act".

In work situation managers have considerable control over the environment or climate in which work is performed. For example, managers design both the monetary reward systems (salaries, bonuses, fringe benefits, and so on). Managers also have much control over the physical aspects of work, such as equipment, tools and buildings.

Selection, training, evaluation and discipline cannot guarantee a high level of employee performance. Motivation, the inner force that directs employee behaviour, also plays an important role. Highly motivated people perform better than unmotivated people. Motivation covers up ability and skill deficiencies in employees. Such truisms about motivation leave employers wanting to be surrounded by highly motivated people but unequipped to motivate their employees.

Employers and supervisors want easily applied motivation models but such models are unavailable.

Motivation probably tops the list of complex activities with which labour managers deal. Their intuition suggests an easy answer, "I want everyone around here to be motivated". They often blame employees for their lack of motivation and performance problems. Employees on the other hand often blame any performance problems they may have on external factors - their supervisors, equipment, training, co-workers, weather, unrealistic demands made on them, pressures at home, lack of recognition etc., etc. Despite the conflicting perceptions held by employers and employees, employers must deal with employee motivation.

Three ways of looking at motivation are: needs, rewards and effort. The needs approach stems from the notion that peoples' unsatisfied needs drive their behaviour. Figure out a person's needs, satisfy the needs and the person will be motivated. For example, a person with a high need to satisfy goals is motivated by production targets. The rewards approach is based on the expectation that rewarded behaviour is repeated. Giving a person a bonus for excellent performance during a difficult harvest period encourages the person to make a special effort during the next difficult harvest. The effort approach to motivation is based on the expectation that effort brings the worker what he or she wants. The thought that working hard leads to advancement and new career opportunities is consistent with the effort approach. The effort approach includes a presumption that the employer is fair, i.e., effort is recognized and rewarded. Managers cannot reduce motivation to a simple choice of one of these approaches. Each of the three approaches contributes to an understanding of motivation and how motivation varies person to person and over time.

The most effective motivation for employees comes from within each employee, i.e., self-motivation. Possible indicators of self-motivation include: past accomplishments in school, sports, organisations and work; stated career goals and other kinds of goals; expertise in one or more areas that shows evidence of craftsmanship, pride in knowledge and abilities, and self-confidence; an evident desire to continue to learn; and a general enthusiasm for life.

Threats, bribery, manipulation and coercion have only limited usefulness beyond the very short-run in changing behaviour in the farm environment. More effective employer action responds to employee needs, making their work useful to satisfying their needs, helping employees understand the relationship between their contribution to success of the farm and rewards received, and creating an atmosphere of equity and fairness.

Theories of Motivation

Motivation theories can generally be divided into motivation theories that focus on needs and Motivation theories that focus on behaviour.

Motivation Theories that Focus on Needs

1. Maslow's need Hierarchy theory of motivation

The need hierarchy theory of motivation was propounded by Abraham Maslow, a clinical psychologist. His theory, which was developed in 1943, represents one of the most widely used theories of the study of motivation in organisations.

Abraham Maslow positioned that the driving force that causes people to join an organisation, remain in it and work towards goals is actually the hierarchy of needs (Maslow, 1970). When the lowest order hierarchy is satisfied, a higher order need appears and since it has the greater potency at the time, this higher-order need causes the individual to attempt to satisfy it. Maslow postulates five basic needs which are shown in figure bellow. In an ascending order, starting with the lowest, the needs are physiological (physical), safety, social,, esteem (ego) and self actualization.

Physiological Needs: The lowest order of human needs consists of the basic physiological necessities such as food, water, shelter and the like. In the less complex societies of the past, it was possible for one to meet these individually or as a participant in relatively primitive organisations. These are the most basic and important of all needs.

Security (safety) needs: once the physiological needs are adequately met, a new level of need which is one step higher in hierarchy (safety need) appears. This need according to Maslow has greater potency and the individual will seek to satisfy it. This need is often met in work organisations through fringe benefits, retirement or pension schemes, insurance benefits, safe working conditions, and so on.

Social needs: if the physical and safety needs are relatively well satisfied, social or love needs will emerge and dominate behaviour. Social needs involve need for social affiliation with other people. It also concerns the need for belongingness, association, affection, friendship, interaction and acceptance in relationship with other people.

Esteem or Ego Needs: Having satisfied the need to belong and to be accepted, the individual has needs to be recognized, to be respected and to have status and prestige. There are two kinds of esteem needs:

(a) Those needs that relate to one's self- esteem– needs for self-confidence, for achievement, for competence and for knowledge.

(b) Those needs that relate to one's reputation -needs for status, recognition, appreciation and deserved respect of one's fellows.

Self-actualization Needs: This in Maslow's view is the highest level of need in the hierarchy and may be described as the desire to become more and more what one is, to become everything that one is capable of becoming. It is often referred as the self-fulfillment need. It concerns the need to maximize the use of one's abilities, skills and realize one's potentialities from self-development, for being creative in the broadest sense of the term.

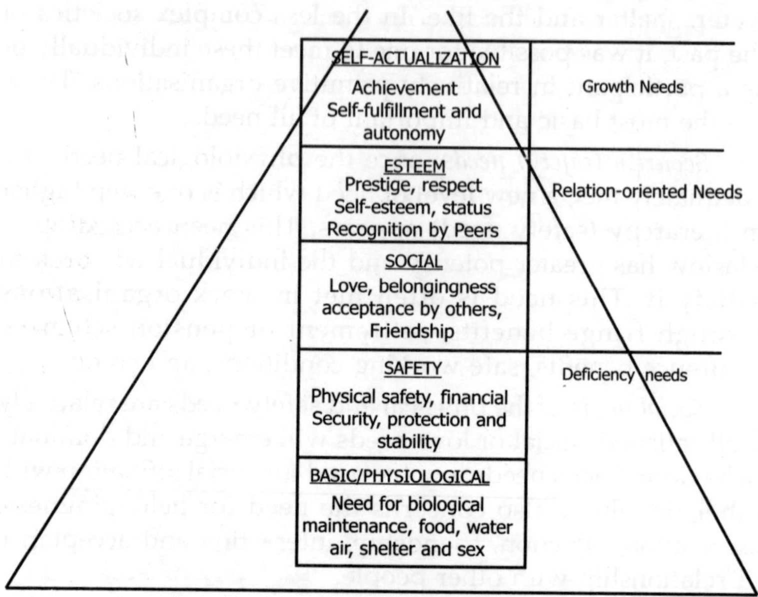

Fig. 7.1: **Maslow's Need Hierarchy**

Source: Kinard, Jerry, Management, D. C. Health and Company, 1988, p. 269 USA.

2. Herzberg: Two- Factor Motivation Theory

The theory called the two-factor or hygiene-motivation theory uncovered two set of factors that lead to job dissatisfaction. According to Herzberg, factors that can produce job dissatisfaction are called hygiene factors. Those that can produce job satisfaction are called motivation factors.

Hygienic or maintenance factors: These are job factors, which are necessary before an individual can be motivated. They are extrinsic to the job-that is they do not relate directly to a person's work. They are part of a job's environment-its context not its content. They do not in themselves inspire or motivate a person to put forth-maximum effort on a job. The hygiene factors include: salary, job security, working conditions, status, quality of technical supervision, quality of interpersonal relations among peers, supervisors and subordinates and organisations policies. Herzberg considers these factors to be hygienic because they are required to have a healthy organisation. The hygiene factors do not motivate people.

Motivation factors/Growth factors: Motivation factors are the primary cause of job satisfaction. They are intrinsic to a job because they relate directly to the real nature (job content) of the work people perform. These include achievement, recognition, advancement, and the possibility for growth and responsibility. Herzberg believes these factors are essential to motivation.

3. McClelland: Need-Based Motivation Theory

David McClelland's theory of motivation states that human beings have three basic motivational needs: power, affiliation, and achievement. The power need is expressed in a strong desire to change or alter the course of events. People who are strongly motivated by the need for power are often effective speakers, may be argumentative, like communicating, and want to exercise influence.

The affiliation exists in all of us but in widely different degrees. Individuals with a strong affiliation need want love and group approval. They value friendship every highly. The needs for affiliation have close interpersonal relationships with peers and individuals working together.

The achievement need is the twin desire to succeed and not fail. McClelland and his colleagues have explored the need of achievement in considerable depth. They have found that people, who have strong achievement need seek challenge, set big goals, work hard and long, and generally want to win for the sake of winning.

Motivation Theories that Focus on Behaviour

1. Vroom: preference- Expectancy theory

Victor Vroom has suggested that motivation relates to two critical factors: preference and expectancy. Preference is what a person wishes to have happen. Expectancy is what a person believes will probably happen if certain behaviour patterns are pursued.

Nothing is more hypocritical than for a manager to say, "we base promotion on performance" and then base it on likeability of the individual or on some other factors that does not relate to actual performance.

2. Skinner's Reinforcement Theory: Motivation Through positive Reinforcement

Skinner's reinforcement theory is based on the belief that all human behaviour is shaped by its consequences. Skinner believes that all behaviour is a result of a reinforcement or stimulus. Behaviour is best modified by deciding what behaviour pattern is desired and then selecting and using the stimulus that produces the desired behaviour.

Skinner recognised three distinct types of reinforcement—positive reinforcement, negative reinforcement, and punishment.

(a) In positive reinforcement, a favorable consequence encourages repetitive behaviour. Examples of positive stimulus include the promise of more money, a promotion, or an assignment to a better job etc.

(b) Negative reinforcement of some behaviour occurs when unpleasant consequences are removed. For example if a worker goes late to work, his supervisor complains. If the worker begins to getting to work on time, the supervisor stops complaining. Eliminating the complaining causes the worker to arrive on time consistently.

(c) In punishment behaviour is changed because it results in unpleasant consequences. Punishment involves inflicting physical or emotional pain or withdrawing a desired consequence. Its purpose is to modify certain behaviour. Examples of negative stimulus include the threat of demotion, lowered pay, or an unwanted transfer etc.

Punishment and reinforcement are not the same. Negative reinforcement involves unpleasant outcomes as punishment does, but it encourages behaviour that avoids unpleasant consequences. Punishment on the other hand, does not encourage action- it suppresses action. This is an important difference. Punishment is used to control what a person should not do.

Skinner is a great believer in positive reinforcement, or rewards, as the best way to achieve desired behaviour. In his view, punishment is likely to produce undesirable behaviour.

3. Reward versus punishment: A component of Most Motivation Theories

By far the oldest-one can say the original theory of motivation calls for rewarding people for "good" behaviour and punishing them for "bad" behaviour. In the adult world of managing, rewards can take many forms-money, bonuses, titles, special office arrangements, awards, more power, entertainment allowances, company cars and so on. Punishment also comes in many forms, such as demotions, undesirable transfer, no pay increases and lack of recognition.

All modern motivation theories stress rewards as a basis for encouraging desired behaviour. Less mention is made, however, of punishment as a motivational tool, since there is no evidence that punishment helps produce more effective or desirable behaviour in the long run. But in general, rewards and punishments are basic to motivation.

4. Equity theory

Equity theory tries to explain the fairness of financial incentive plans. According to the equity theory of pay, a person looks at the relationship between what she or he puts into work and what she or he gets out of it in comparison with that of other workers. This comparison is more important to a worker than is the direct relationship between performance and reward. This is considered to be the central factor in determining the effectiveness of a pay plan. Equity exists whenever the formula is in balance:

$$\frac{\text{Individual A's outcome}}{\text{Individual A's input}} = \frac{\text{Other workers' outcome}}{\text{Other workers' input}}$$

Inequity exists if one side of the equation greater than the other. The worker who sees this imbalance wants to reduce her or his feeling of inequity. Equity theory is based on the assumption that people are motivated by a desire to be equitably treated at work If the left side of the equation is greater than the right side, the individual is over-rewarded and If the left side of the equation is less than the right side, the individual is under-rewarded.

Other Motivation Related Theories

1. Likert: participative-Management Approach

Rensis Likert and his associates have spent decades in shading light on the question" What management style gets the best results? Likert tried to determine whether highly autocratic management, ("do it in my way") or, at other extreme participate management ("what ideas do you have for getting the job done?") works best.

Generally, Likert's research shows that managers who practice effective human relations by letting lower-level personnel participate in making decisions that affect them achieve better cooperation, higher motivation, and greater productivity. He found that people who do the work want to be consulted about how to do it.

2. Mayo: The Hawthorne Effect

G. Elton Mayo, a Harvard psychologist, conducted an extensive study of worker motivation at the Hawthorne plant of the western Electric Company in the 1930s. In his experiments, Mayo modified the density of lights in the work area, pay scales, amount of rest time, and other environmental factors to determine the effects of these changes on productivity.

Surprisingly, productivity of the workers in the study went up even when working conditions worsened. Mayo discovered that worker's productivity increases when special attention is focused on them; the attention gives them special status among their peers. His study showed that workers' attitudes are key to their motivation-and fair treatment improves their attitudes. Workers resent being taken for granted and treated like machines.

THE ROLE OF COMMUNICATION IN MANAGEMENT

Purposes of Communication

Communication is one of the manager's most important tools. When used correctly, it embodies the speaker's objectives and helps accomplish tasks that require coordination. Besides important social uses, communication has four functions in business:

1. Disseminating information;
2. Motivating and persuading;
3. Promoting understanding; and
4. Aiding in decision-making.

The first three purposes of communication are obvious; less apparent is the role of communication in decision making.

Communication is an important part of the decision-making process. Many times, only a unified opinion will get results. Other times, the varying opinions of different organisational members form the basis for a decision. And in some cases, decisions reflect nothing more than the opinion of the most demanding or most articulate participant.

The Communication Process

The fundamental elements of the communication process include: the speaker, the message, and the audience. These elements of communication which were first recognized by Aristotle before twenty-five centuries (Figure 7.2) are also the focus of modern communication theory.

Fig. 7.2: Aristotelian Model of Communication

Source: Kinard, Jerry, Management, D. C. Health and Company, 1988, p. 349 USA.

In recent years, the model has been modified to include the findings of behaviourists and other psychologists. Other models reflect technological innovations and interpersonal communication. Phillip Lewis's model, illustrated in Figure 7.3, shows how communication occurs in a formal organisation. This diagram shows that organisational communication is a complex system involving people's feelings, attitudes, relationships, and skills as well as the goals of management and the process of change, adaptation, and growth. Individuals can both send and receive information. Both the receiver and sender have their own personal frame of reference, developed over time. Lewis's model, which is relevant for both formal and informal communication, represents upward, downward, and horizontal transmissions of information.

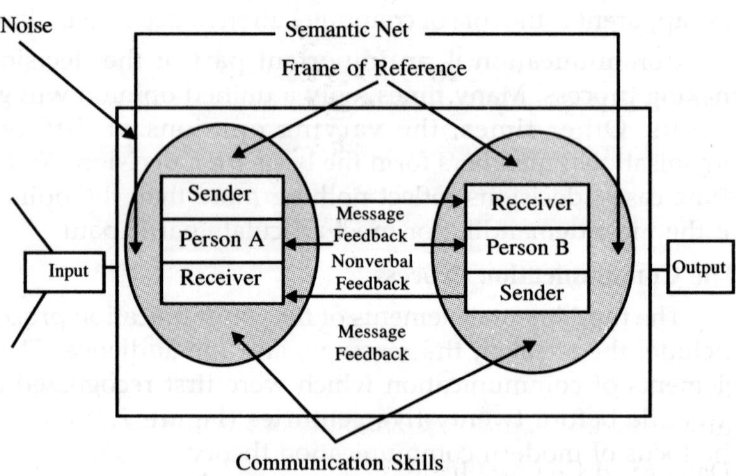

***Fig. 7.3:* Lewis's Organisational Communication Model**

Source: Kinard, Jerry, Management, D. C. Health and Company, 1988, p. 350 USA.

Verbal and Nonverbal Feedback

The communication process in Figure 8.11 depicts a manager sending a written or oral message to another organisational member through a channel. The receiver accepts the message and transmits either verbal or nonverbal feedback, thereby becoming the sender. It is important to understand the difference between verbal feedback, nonverbal feedback, and noise.

(a) *Verbal feedback* is a written or spoken response.

(b) *Nonverbal feedback* is body movement or actions.

(c) *Noise* is the interference or the barriers that may occur at any point in the process, distorting understanding.

The organisational environment also affects sending, receiving, and interpreting the message. The communication process is successful only when the sender and receiver understand the message to the same degree. Feedback permits clarification and repetition until the message is fully understood.

Organisational Communication: A Linking Process

The information flow is essential to an organisation's effectiveness. Several studies have shown that many work-related problems are caused by poor attitudes rather than by inadequate skills and knowledge. Open communication moulds positive attitudes and improves the likelihood of job satisfaction and better job performance. In all organisations, formal and informal information is transmitted through different channels. These channels are categorized as downward, upward, horizontal and vertical.

Downward Communication

Downward communication occurs when information is transmitted from higher to lower levels in an organisation. Directives, policy statements, and memoranda fall into this category. Katz and Kahn identify five major types of down ward-flowing information:

1. *Job instructions,* which explain how a task is to be performed. They come from written specifications, training manuals, training sessions, or on the-job training.
2. *Job rationale statements,* which explain to workers how their tasks relate to other jobs in the company. Specialization in many organisations has made it difficult to see how their particular tasks fit into the overall operations of the firm. Job rationale communications answer this problem.
3. *Policy and procedure statements,* which explain the employer's regulations and personal benefits provided.
4. *Feedback,* which includes messages that tell employees whether their work is satisfactory. Feedback should be provided daily, as well as in the form of periodic performance appraisal.
5. *Indoctrination communications,* which try to drum up employees' support for a particular organisational goal, such as an area fund-raising drive.

Upward Communication

Upward communication is the flow of opinions, ideas, complaints, and other kinds of information from subordinates up to managers. It is generated by suggestion systems, grievance procedures, informal and formal meetings, attitude surveys, and exit interviews. Upward communication is important for several reasons.

(a) Managers need to know how their subordinates feel about their jobs, their working conditions, and the company's policies and procedures.
(b) Upward communication encourages workers to discuss particular job-related problems that may be hindering productivity and efficiency.
(c) It provides managers with feedback on the workers' reactions on the policy changes, developments in their departments, and other matters that affect their attitudes and performance. In other words, upward communication supplies management with the information that it needs to make intelligent decision.

There is another spin-off benefit of upward communication as well. Whenever workers are encouraged to communicate with upper-level managers, downward communication, such as policy changes, meets with less resistance.

Managers who isolate themselves from what is happening below them are asking for trouble. Besides losing such reality, they fail to maintain close rapport with their subordinates. In many instances, isolation results when a manager refuses to listen to his or her subordinates or has inadequate personal interaction with them. Workers feel isolated when they think that their boss doesn't want to be bothered with their problems.

Horizontal Communication

Horizontal, or lateral, communication refers to the flow of information among workers on the same organisational level. Kinard, Jerry (1988) said that horizontal channels can be used for:

(a) Coordinating tasks,
(b) Solving problems
(c) Sharing information,
(d) Resolving conflict, and
(e) Developing rapport among workers.

Horizontal communication is essential for managers and workers alike. Without it, business functions could not be coordinated. Sound decision-making also relies on information sharing among functional units. Several studies have shown that most poor management decisions result from poor communication. Effective organisations also need horizontal communication.

People who work closely together and communicate regularly rarely have difficulty understanding one another. Their interaction also provides emotional support and helps satisfy their social needs. Even so, formal horizontal communication channels often do not give employees all the information they want. As a result, informal channels-commonly called the grapevine-develop. What is grapevine?

Vertical Communication

Vertical communication may be upward or downward communication. As can be understood from the previous discussion, organisations not only generate internal communication but communication flows within an organisation are multilateral. Vertical (upward and downward) communication flows are the primary considerations in organisational design. When we think of communicating, we usually visualize messages being sent vertically downward from one level to lower levels by way of the chain of command. This is the path that most orders and instructions take. But much communicating is vertically upward, from lower to higher levels. Managers require information from their subordinates about their problems, work in progress and other data that relate to what the organisation is doing.

Informal Communication Channels-The Grapevine

The rumour mill known as the grapevine is the informal communication network that is responsible for transmitting an astonishing five out of every six messages in organisations. This network is the informal communication system for the organisation and also supplements the formal communication network. The grapevine is a natural phenomenon that can provide social satisfaction, power, and prestige to workers. Messages may be factual or inaccurate. Rumours often start with people who are in a spot for seeing and hearing things but are not necessarily in high organisational positions. For instance, a secretary may overhear a conversation, or a custodian may see a discarded message. From such small seeds, the grapevine grows.

Characteristics of the Grapevine

Kinard, Jerry (1988), describes characteristics of the grapevine and the different networks for transmitting information via the grapevine as follows.

The characteristics of the grapevine include:

(a) Spread information rapidly;

(b) Was selective in terms of what was transmitted;

(c) Filled voids left by the formal communication channels; and

(d) Was confined to the workplace.

Obstacles to Effective Communication

The primary objective of communication is to make the message under-stood. Secondary objectives include securing a response (feedback) that is either positive, negative, or noncommittal and maintaining favourable relation-ships with people with whom we communicate. But it so happens that we often fail to communicate effectively; our efforts falter because of obstacles and barriers inhibiting the communication process. The major obstacles in the communication process are: Semantic Problems, Varying Perception, Filtering, Poor Listening Habits, Too Many Organisational Levels, Lack of Credibility, Kinetics (Body languages), Low Readership Level, and Psychological Communication Barriers.

Barriers to Communication

Problems with any one of the components of the communication model can become a barrier to communication. These barriers suggest opportunities for improving communication.

1. *Muddled messages:* Effective communication starts with a clear message. Contrast these two messages: "Please be here about 7:00 tomorrow morning." "Please be here at 7:00 tomorrow morning." The one word difference makes the first message muddled and the second message clear. Muddled messages are a barrier to communication because the receiver is left unclear about the intent of the sender. Muddled messages have many causes. The sender may be confused in his or her thinking. The message may be little more than a vague idea. The problem may be semantics, e.g., note this muddled newspaper ad: "Dog

for sale. Will eat anything. Especially likes children. Call 888-3599 for more information."

Feedback from the receiver is the best way for a sender to be sure that the message is clear rather than muddled. Clarifying muddled messages is the responsibility of the sender. The sender hoping the receiver will figure out what was really meant does little to remove this barrier to communication.

2. *Stereotyping:* Stereotyping causes us to typify a person, a group, an event or a thing on oversimplified conceptions, beliefs, or opinions. Thus, basketball players can be typed as tall, green equipment as better than red equipment, football linemen as dumb, Ford as better than Chevrolet, Vikings as handsome, and people raised on swine farms as interested in animals. Stereotyping can substitute for thinking, analysis and open mindedness to a new situation.

   Stereotyping is a barrier to communication when it causes people to act as if they already know the message that is coming from the sender or worse, as if no message is necessary because "everybody already knows." Both senders and listeners should continuously look for and address thinking, conclusions and actions based on stereotypes.

3. *Wrong channel:* "Good morning." An oral channel for this message is highly appropriate. Writing "GOOD MORNING!" on a chalk board in the machine shed is less effective than a warm oral greeting. On the other hand, a detailed request to a contractor for construction of a farrowing house should be in writing, i.e., non-oral. A long conversation between a pork producer and a contractor about the farrowing house construction, with neither taking notes, surely will result in confusion and misunderstanding. Similarly, several conversations between a father and son concerning a partnership and long-term plans for the business, with neither taking notes,

surely will result in confusion and misunderstanding. It will also likely result in other family members not understanding what father and son have agreed to. These simple examples illustrate how the wrong channel can be a barrier to communication.

Variation of channels helps the receiver understand the nature and importance of a message. Using a training video on cleaning practices helps new employees grasp the importance placed on herd health. A written disciplinary warning for tardiness emphasizes to the employee that the problem is serious. A birthday card to a daughter-in-law is more sincere than a request to a son to say "Happy Birthday" to his wife.

Simple rules for selection of a channel cause more problems than they solve. In chosing a channel, the sender needs to be sensitive to such things as the complexity of the message (good morning versus a construction contract); the consequences of a misunderstanding (medication for a sick animal versus a guess about tomorrow's weather); knowledge, skills and abilities of the receiver (a new employee versus a partner in the business); and immediacy of action to be taken from the message (instructions for this morning's work versus a plan of work for next year).

4. *Language:* Words are not reality. Words as the sender understands them are combined with the perceptions of those words by the receiver. Language represents only part of the whole. We fill in the rest with perceptions. Trying to understand a foreign language easily demonstrates words not being reality. Being "foreign" is not limited to the language of another country. It can be the language of another farm. The Gerken house may be where the Browns now live. The green goose may be a trailer painted red long after it was given the name green goose. A brassy day may say much about temperature and little about color.

Each new family member and employee needs to be taught the language of the farm. Until the farm's language is learned, it can be as much a barrier to communication as a foreign language.

5. *Lack of feedback:* Feedback is the mirror of communication. Feedback mirrors what the sender has sent. Feedback is the receiver sending back to the sender the message as perceived. Without feedback, communication is one-way.

   Feedback happens in a variety of ways. Asking a person to repeat what has been said, e.g., repeat instructions, is a very direct way of getting feedback. Feedback may be as subtle as a stare, a puzzled look, a nod, or failure to ask any questions after complicated instructions have been given. Both sender and receiver can play an active role in using feedback to make communication truly two-way.

   Feedback should be helpful rather than hurtful. Prompt feedback is more effective that feedback saved up until the "right" moment. Feedback should deal in specifics rather than generalities. Approach feedback as a problem in perception rather than a problem of discovering the facts.

6. *Poor listening skills:* Listening is difficult. A typical speaker says about 125 words per minute. The typical listener can receive 400-600 words per minute. Thus, about 75 per cent of listening time is free time. The free time often sidetracks the listener. The solution is to be an active rather than passive listener.

   One important listening skill is to be prepared to listen. Tune out thoughts about other people and other problems. Search for meaning in what the person is saying. A mental outline or summary of key thoughts can be very helpful. Avoid interrupting the speaker. "Shut up" is a useful listening guideline. "Shut up some more" is a useful extension of this guideline. Withhold evaluation and judgement until the other person has finished with the message. A listener's premature frown, shaking of the head, or bored look can easily convince the other person there is no reason to elaborate or try again to communicate his or her excellent idea.

Providing feedback is the most important active listening skill. Ask questions. Nod in agreement. Look the person straight in the eye. Lean forward. Be an animated listener. Focus on what is being said. Repeat key points.

Active listening is particularly important in dealing with an angry person. Encouraging the person to speak, i.e., to vent feelings, is essential to establishing communication with an angry person. Repeat what the person has said. Ask questions to encourage the person to say again what he or she seemed most anxious to say in the first place. An angry person will not start listening until they have "cooled" down. Telling an angry person to "cool" down often has the opposite effect. Getting angry with an angry person only assures that there are now two people not listening to what the other is saying.

7. *Interruptions:* A farm is a lively place. Few days are routine. Long periods of calm and quiet rarely interrupt the usual hectic pace. In this environment, conversations, meetings, instructions and even casual talk about last night's game are likely to be interrupted. The interruptions may be due to something more pressing, rudeness, lack of privacy for discussion, a drop-in visitor, an emergency or even the curiosity of someone else wanting to know what two other people are talking about.

   No matter the cause, interruptions are a barrier to communication. In the extreme, there is a reluctance of employees and family members even to attempt discussion with a manager because of the near certainty that the conversation will be interrupted. Less extreme but nevertheless serious is the problem of incomplete instructions because someone came by with a pressing question.

8. *Physical distractions:* Physical distractions are the physical things that get in the way of communication. Examples of such things include the telephone, a pick-up truck door, a desk, an uncomfortable meeting place, and noise.

   These physical distractions are common on farms. If the phone rings, the tendency is to answer it even if the caller is interrupting a very important or even delicate conversation. A supervisor may give instructions from the driver's seat of a pick-up truck. Talking through an open window and down to an employee makes the truck door a barrier. A person sitting behind a desk, especially if sitting in a large chair, talking across the desk is talking from behind a physical barrier. Two people talking facing each other without a desk or truck-door between them have a much more open and personal sense of communication. Uncomfortable meeting places may include a place on the farm that is too hot or too cold. Another example is a meeting room with uncomfortable chairs that soon cause people to want to stand even if it means cutting short the discussion. Noise is a physical distraction simply because it is hard to concentrate on a conversation if hearing is difficult.

Facilitating Communication

Beyond removal of specific barriers to communication, the following general guidelines may also help communication.

1. Have a positive attitude about communication. Defensiveness interferes with communication.
2. Work at improving communication skills. It takes knowledge and work. The communication model and discussion of barriers to communication provide the necessary knowledge. This increased awareness of the potential for improving communication is the first step to better communication.
3. Include communication as a skill to be evaluated along with all the other skills in each person's job description.

Help other people improve their communication skills by helping them understand their communication problems.

4. Make communication goal oriented. Relational goals come first and pave the way for other goals. When the sender and receiver have a good relationship, they are much more likely to accomplish their communication goals.
5. Approach communication as a creative process rather than simply part of the chore of working with people. Experiment with communication alternatives. What works with one person may not work well with another person. Vary channels, listening techniques and feedback techniques.
6. Accept the reality of miscommunication. The best communicators fail to have perfect communication. They accept miscommunication and work to minimize its negative impacts.

Controlling

Controlling establishes performance standards used to measure progress toward goals. The purpose of controlling is to determine whether people and the various parts of an organisation are on target, achieving the progress toward their objectives that they planned to achieve. Planning chooses goals and maps out the necessary strategy and tactics. Controlling attempts to prevent failure (and to promote success) by providing the means to monitor the performances of individuals, departments, divisions, and the entire organisation.

Stoner, James A.F. and Freeman R. Edward (1992) define management control as a systematic effort to set performance standards with planning objectives, to design information feedback systems, to compare actual performance with these predetermined standards, and to determine whether there are any deviations and to measure their significance and to take any action required to assure that all organisational resources are used in the most effective and efficient way possible in achieving organisational objectives.

The Control Process

The planning process determines objectives that eventually become the foundation for controls. Planning the first function is the heart of all the others. The control process consists of four basic steps applicable to any persons, items, or processes being controlled.

These steps are as follows:

1. Establish standards or targets.
2. Measuring actual performance
3. Comparing actual performance against standards
4. Take actions necessary to correct deviations from standards.

1. Establishing Standards

Standards are derived from objectives and have many of the same characteristics. Like objectives, standards are targets; to be effective, they must be stated clearly and be related logically to objectives. Standards are the criteria that enable managers to evaluate future, current, or past actions. Standards are units of measurement established by management to serve as benchmarks for comparing performance levels. A standard is a measuring device, quantitative or qualitative, that is designed to help monitor the performance of people, capital goods, or processes. The exact nature of the standards to be used depends on what is being monitored. Standards can take different forms. Standards for comparison can apply to personnel, marketing, production, financial operations, and so on. The various forms standards take depend on *what* is being measured and on *the managerial level responsible* for taking corrective action. Whatever the standards, however, they all can be assigned to one of two groups: managerial standards or technical standards.

2. Measuring Actual Performance

The first step in the control process has established the measuring device. The second step asks managers and others to measure the performance. The way that standards are expressed may define how they should be measured. Profitability standards, for example, imply that the measuring unit is Birr. Quantity standards are typically defined in terms of physical unit of output.

3. Comparing Performance against Standards

In possession of clear, simple standards that outline the acceptable and the unacceptable, managers can apply the standards to specific performances. This application often asks that comparisons be made between the 'what is' and "what should be". Actual output or performance that does not precisely conform to standards may still be 'in control'. A slight departure from standards (acceptable) is normal and expected; however, gross departure from standards (unacceptable) signal the need for immediate corrective action. A manager needs to distinguish between acceptable variation and variation indicating that the process is out of control. If the comparison yields results or measurements that are acceptable – within prescribed limits - no action need be taken. If the results show a trend away from the acceptable or, show the unacceptable, action may be called for. Measurements must be taken regularly to discover any deviations as quickly as possible.

The purpose of a manager's comparing past performance with planned performance is not only to determine when an error has been made but also to predict future outcomes. A good control system, then, will provide quick comparisons so the manager can detect possible trouble while the operation is still under control. Comparisons of actual performance over time often will show a trend that might be a danger signal. The manager cannot change the past, but the knowledge of the past will help her or him make the right decision today that will affect tomorrow.

4. Taking Corrective Action

To correct is to amend; remedy, rectify, or in some other way make right what is wrong. The objective of corrective action is to 'get things back on track' so that standards are met or, if they cannot be met, then to set new standards.

Let us now assume that management has noted a deviation from a standard. A cause or causes for the deviation have been determined. Now, determining the precise action to take will depend on:

(a) the standard;

(b) the accuracy of the measurements that determined that a deviation exists; and

(c) the diagnosis of the person or device investigating the cause for the deviation.

Standards can be too loose or too strict. Measurements may be inaccurate because of poor use of measuring devices or defects in the devices themselves. Finally, people can use poor judgment in determining the corrective actions to be taken.

Corrective actions can be prescribed by management in advance through polices, procedures, and practices. When such prescriptions exist, they help to shorten the reaction times to problems. But not every situation involving deviations from standards can be cured with a prescribed solution.

Great care must be taken in the most important step in the process of taking corrective action: detecting the causes for deviations. It is often easy to assume that we know what is wrong and why. But how often have we attempted to solve a problem that didn't exist at all? We have to remember that several diseases have the same symptoms; hence, failure to meet a goal may have more than one cause, each of which or may, require a unique solution.

Types of Control

What types of controls are there, and what is their purpose? Work formed by organisations and their employees has a starting point (where inputs take place), a period of performance (where the inputs are meshed), and a final product (or output). Figure 8.1 showed this processing of work as a continuous system. Because of the nature of work and work flow various types of controls have been developed. There are three basic of controls: prevention, feed forward, and feedback. Each type of control has its place helping plans reach their potential.

Prevention Controls (Pre-control)

The old maxim an ounce of prevention is better than a pound of cure does hold true when a business security or security of human being is involved. Better to prevent trouble than have to deal with its related problems. Prevention controls methods increase the possibility that future actual results will compare favorably with planned results. Prevention controls focus on establishing conditions that will make it difficult or impossible for deviations from norms to occur. Policies are important prevention control methods since they define appropriate future action. Other precontrol methods involve human, capital, and financial resources.

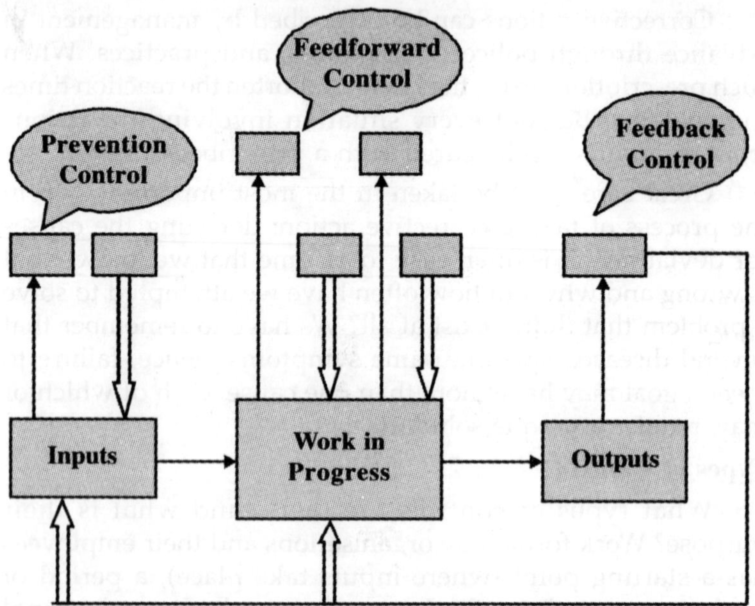

Fig. 8.1: **Types of Controls (Prevention, Feedforward, and Feedback Controls)**

Source: Plunkett, Warren R., and Attner, Raymond F., Introduction to Management; USA Kent Publishing Co. Boston, 1989 p. 365, USA.

Human resources: Precontrol of *human resources* depends on job requirements. Job requirements predetermine the skills needed by the job holders. How specific the skills must be will depend on the nature of the task. At the shop level, for example, the skills needed may include specific physical attributes and degrees of manual dexterity. On the other hand, the job requirements for management and staff personnel can be more difficult to define with concrete measurements.

Capital Resources: The acquisition of *capital* reflects the need to replace existing equipment or to expand the firm's productive capacity. Capital acquisitions can be precontrolled by establishing criteria of potential profitability that must be met before the acquisitions are authorized. Decisions involving the commitment of present funds in exchange for future funds are termed *investment decisions*. Control methods that screen investment proposals are derived from financial analysis.

Financial Resources: Adequate *financial* resources must be available to ensure the payment of obligations arising from current operations. Materials must be purchased, wages paid, and interest charges and due dates met. Budgets – particularly cash and working capital budgets – are the principal means for precontrolling the availability and cost of financial resources. These budgets anticipate the ebb and flow of business activity when materials are purchased, finished goods are produced, goods are sold, and cash is received. This cycle of activity, the operating cycle, results in a problem of *timing* the availability of cash to meet the obligations. As inventories of finished goods increase, material, labour, and other expenses are incurred and paid, and the supply of cash decreases. As inventory is sold, the supply of cash increases. Precontrol of cash requires that funds be available during the period of inventory buildup, and that cash be used wisely during periods of abundance.

Feedforward Controls (Concurrent Controls)

Prevention controls focus on establishing conditions that will make it difficult or impossible for deviations to occur and are therefore generally placed at the start of a process; they block or disarm trouble. Feedforward controls, however, are future directed: They are designed to detect and anticipate deviations from standards at various points throughout the process. They are in-process controls. Feedforward controls are often called steering controls because they allow people to act on a process or activity proceeding, not after it is completed. Corrections and adjustment can be made as the need arises. There are two kinds of feedforward control devices: diagnostic and therapeutic.

Diagnostic controls attempt to determine what deviation is taking or has taken place. They tell you what is wrong – not why. Diagnosis makes use of measurements that rely on the five senses. Perhaps the best kind of diagnosis occurs when the person most familiar with a situation uses his or her intuition and background experiences in discovering what has gone wrong. A physician's first line of attack on a patient's complaints involves that bank of previously acquired knowledge. Tests and other checks may be called on later to verify what the physician believes to be the proper diagnosis.

Therapeutic controls sense both the "what" and the "why", and then they take corrective action.

Concurrent control consists primarily of actions by supervisors who direct the work of their subordinates. *Direction* refers to the acts managers undertake

1. To instruct subordinates in the proper methods and procedures and
2. To oversee the work of subordinates to ensure that it is done properly.

Direction follows the formal chain of command, since the responsibility of each manager is to interpret for subordinates the orders received from higher echelons. The relative importance of direction depends almost entirely on the nature of the tasks performed by subordinates.

Feedback Controls (Postcontrol)

Feedback controls are postaction controls and focus on the end results of the process. The information derived is not used for corrective action on a project because it has been completed. The feedback control provides information for a manager to examine and apply to future activities that are similar to the present one. The purpose is to help prevent mistakes in the future. Four postconrol methods are widely used in business: financial statement analysis, standard cost analysis, employee performance evaluation, and quality control.

Financial statement analysis: A firm's accounting system is a principal source of information from which managers can evaluate historical results. Periodically, managers receive *financial statements*, which usually include a balance sheet, an income statement, and a sources-and-uses-of-funds statement. These statements summarize and classify the effects of transactions in terms of assets, liabilities, equity, revenues, and expenses – the principal components of the firm's financial structure.

Standard cost analysis: *Standard cost accounting* systems are a major contribution of scientific management. A standard cost system provides information that enables management to compare actual costs with predetermined (standard) costs. Management then can take appropriate corrective action or assign others the authority to take action. The first uses of standard cost accounting were concerned with manufacturing costs.

Employee performance evaluation: The most difficult postcontrol method is *performance evaluation*. Yet good performance evaluation is important, because people are the most crucial resource in any organisation. Effective business firms, hospitals, universities, and governments must have people who are effectively performing their assigned duties. Evaluating performance can be very difficult, however, because the standards for performance seldom are objective and straightforward. Furthermore, many managerial and nonmanagerial jobs do not produce outputs that can be counted, weighed, and evaluated in objective terms.

Each control method, whether precontrol, concurrent control, or postcontrol, requires the same four fundamental elements: standards, measuring actual performance, comparing actual performance and standard and corrective action. Of the four, measuring actual performance and comparing actual performance which generate information is the element most critical for effective control. Managers act on the basis of information – reports, documents, position papers, and analyses. Without information, standards could not be set, and corrective action could not be taken.

The precontrol, concurrent control or postcontrol methods are not mutually exclusive. Rather they are usually combined into an integrated control system. Such a control system for standards, measuring actual performance, comparing actual performance and standard and taking corrective action can be performed at every point from input to output.

How to Make Controls Effective

Controls are effective as long as:

1. they do what they are intended for – prevent deviations, diagnose deviations, treat deviations, or provide information for future planning;
2. they do not create organisational problems that result in costs greater than the benefits of the control devices.

Forms of Controls/Control Techniques

1. ***General management controls:***
    - The management information system.
    - Key Indicator Management.
    - Human asset accounting.
    - Inventory control systems.
2. ***Special control techniques***
    - Financial Controls
    - Budgets
    - Financial Statements
    - The balance sheet
    - The income statement
    - Ratios
    - Audits
    - Management audit

3. ***Production controls***
   - Gantt Charts
   - Programme evaluation review technique (PERT)
   - Quality Control
   - Computers and controls
4. ***Other techniques of control***
   - Planning, programming, budgeting systems (PPBS)
   - Personal observation
   - Client or customer satisfaction questionnaires:
   - Performance appraisal
   - Breakeven Analysis

Characteristics of the Control Process

The control process is cyclical which means it is never finished. Controlling leads to identification of new problems that in turn need to be addressed through establishment of performance standards, measuring performance etc.

Employees often view controlling negatively. By its very nature, controlling often leads to management expecting employee behaviour to change. No matter how positive the changes may be for the organisation, employees may still view them negatively.

Control is both anticipatory and retrospective. The process anticipates problems and takes preventive action. With corrective action, the process also follows up on problems.

Ideally, each person in the business views control as his or her responsibility. The organisational culture should prevent a person walking away from a small, easily solvable problem because "that isn't my responsibility." In customer driven businesses, each employee cares about each customer. In quality driven dairy farms, for example, each employee cares about the welfare of each animal and the wear and tear on each piece of equipment.

Controlling is related to each of the other functions of management. Controlling builds on planning, organizing and leading.

Management Control Strategies

Managers can use one or a combination of three control strategies or styles: market, bureaucracy and clan. Each serves a different purpose. External forces make up market control. Without external forces to bring about needed control, managers can turn to internal bureaucratic or clan control. The first relies primarily on budgets and rules. The second relies on employees wanting to satisfy their social needs through feeling a valued part of the business.

Self-control, sometimes called adhocracy control, is complementary to market, bureaucratic and clan control. By training and encouraging individuals to take initiative in addressing problems on their own, there can be a resulting sense of individual empowerment. This empowerment plays out as self-control. The self-control then benefits the organisation and increases the sense of worth to the business in the individual.

Designing Effective Control Systems

Effective control systems have the following characteristics:

1. Control at all levels in the business
2. Acceptability to those who will enforce decisions
3. Flexibility
4. Accuracy
5. Timeliness
6. Cost effectiveness
7. Understandability
8. Balance between objectivity and subjectivity
9. Coordinated with planning, organising and leading

Dysfunctional Consequences of Control

Managers expect people in an organisation to change their behaviour in response to control. However, employee resistance can easily make control efforts dysfunctional. The following behaviours demonstrate means by which the manager's control efforts can be frustrated:

1. Game playing → control is something to be beaten, a game between the "boss and me and I want to win."
2. Resisting control → a "blue flu" reaction to too much control.
3. Providing inaccurate information → a lack of understanding of why the information is needed and important leading to "you want numbers, we will give you numbers."
4. Following rules to the letter → people following dumb and unprofitable rules in reaction to "do as I say."
5. Sabotaging → stealing, discrediting other workers, chasing customers away, gossiping about the firm to people in the community.
6. Playing one manager off against another → exploiting lack of communication among managers, asking a second manager if don't like the answer from the first manager.

Glossary

Accountability Being answerable for the results of one's action.

Advise impact The effect a selection device has when it excludes a significantly greater number of minority group members or women than other Groups.

Alternative A potential course of action that is likely to eliminate, correct or neutralise the cause of a problem.

Assumptions The premises or condition that planners accept as or know to be true and real because of their experiences or those of others.

Authority The right to make decision that commit the organisation's resources or the legal right of a manager to tell someone to do or not to do something, also called formal or positional authority.

Brainstorming A group effort at generating ideas and alternatives, using inside experts who focus on one issue or problem.

Breakeven analysis A quantitative planning technique relating costs, revenue and profit. It determines at what point income and expenses are equal where organisation breaks even.

Budget A single-use plan for predicting, sources and amounts of income and how it is to be used.

Budgeting A planning technique that attempts to formalize in writing the financial resources to be allocated for specific purposes.

Chain of command The organising principle concerned with the number of management positions in an organisation and their unbroken connection to its top position.

Committee A group of people who volunteer or are appointed to serve as investigators, problem solvers, or decision makers.

Communication The transmission of information and understanding from one person or group to another.

Communication barriers Objects or behaviours that ca interfere with communication effectiveness.

Conceptual skill The ability to view the organisation as a whole and see how the parts of the organisation relate and depends on one another. Deals with ideas and abstractions.

Contingency model A theory of leadership (of Fielder) that holds that the effectiveness of a leader is determined by the interaction of the leader behavior (orientation) and three

	variables: leader-member relations, task structure, and leader position power.
Continuum of leadership behaviour	Tannenbaum and Schmidt's visual representation of the various possible leadership approaches: the choice of one depends on the amount decision-making the leader is willing or able to share with subordinates. Positions along the continuum range from autocratic to free-rein approaches.
Controlling	Establishing performance standards used to measure progress toward goals.
Crisis team	Key people located throughout the organisation who come together in an emergency to take charge and make the necessary decisions to deal with tits impact on the organisation.
Critical path	The longest path through a production flowchart or diagram from start to finish.
Decision	The result of making judgment or reaching a conclusion.
Decision making	A rational choice among alternative-making a judgment or reaching a conclusion.
Decision tree	A graphic presentation of the actions a manager can take and how these actions relate to further events.
Delegation	The downward transfer of formal authority from one person to another.
Delphi technique	forecasting technique using the opinions of outside experts.

Demotion The movement from one position to another that has less pay or responsibility attached to it.

Departmentation The creation of groups, subdivision, or departments that will execute and oversee the various tasks that management considers essential.

Diagnostic control A monitoring device or system that attempts to determine what deviation from a standard from a standard is taking or has taken place.

Division of labour The study of tasks deemed essential, the breaking down of tasks into parts or steps, and the assigning of one or more of those parts to an individual or position.

Equity theory A motivation theory stating that people are influenced in their behavior choices (motivation) through the comparison of relative input-outcome ratios. People compare the ratios of their input (efforts) with outcome (rewards) to others' ratios to see if equity exists.

Expectancy theory A motivation theory stating that a person's behaviour is influenced by the value of the rewards, the relationship of the rewards to the performance necessary, and the effort required for performance.

Feedback A receiver's reaction to a message, through which a receiver becomes a sender.

Feedback control A monitoring device or system deigned to detect and to anticipate

	deviations from standards at various points throughout ongoing processes.
Fixed costs	Costs unconnected to and separate from the costs of manufacturing a product or selling it.
Forecast	Planners' expectation about the likely of probable state of events or conditions at some time in the future.
Functional authority	Authority over specific activities that are undertaken by personnel in other departments.
Game theory	An operations research technique that attempts to predict how people or organisations will behave in competitive situations.
Human skill	The ability to interact with other people successfully. To understand, work with, and relate to individuals and to groups of people.
Hygiene factors	Herzberg's list of causes most closely identified with unhappiness of the job. These extrinsic factors, if provided in the right qualities by management, can result in no job dissatisfaction.
Impersonal communication	Communication in which the participants do not interact directly.
Induction	Providing a person entering a company with the necessary information about the company.
Interpersonal communication	Communication delivered in either a face-to-face or voice-to-voice method.
Job enlargement	Increases in the variety of the number of tasks a job includes, not the quality or the challenge of those tasks.

Job enrichment Designing a job to provide more responsibility, control, feedback, and authority for decision-making.

Job rotation Sending people to different jobs on a rotating or temporary basis.

Leadership The process of influencing the group or individual toward the accomplishment of goal setting or goal achievement.

Life cycle A theory or leadership that states that the leadership approach varies with the maturity of the individual. An employee's maturity is viewed as his or her task-related ability and experience as well as willingness to accept responsibility.

Limiting factors Constraints managers work with that rule out potential alternatives.

Line authority Direct supervisory authority from superior to subordinate.

Line departments Departments established to meet the major objectives of the organisation.

Linear programming A quantitative planning technique that attempts to determine the best way to allocate resources when given the possible alternative uses for and limitations on the resources.

Management The process of setting and achieving goals through the execution of five basic management functions that utilise human, financial and material resources.

Management by objectives (MBO) An approach to appraisals that requires subordinates to negotiate goals along with priorities and timetables for them I concert with their superiors.

Managerial grid Blake and Mouton's visual representation of possible leadership behaviors, of which the one that occurs will result form the leader's orientation toward task or toward employee. A balance between the two extremes of orientation most often yields the most effective management behaviour.

Managers Those in positions of authority who make decisions to commit resources toward the achievement of goals.

Maximize Make the best possible decision. Requires ideal resources information, time, personnel, equipment and supplies.

Medium The method chosen to deliver a message.

Message The information being transmitted in the communication process.

Mission The formal statement about the central purpose behind the organisation's existence-its reason to be.

Motivation The interaction of a person's internalised need and external influences (equity, expectancy, and previous conditioning) that determines behavior designed to achieve a goal.

Motivation factors Herzberg's list of conditions that can lead to an individual's job satisfaction. Thy are intrinsic to the job and offer satisfactions for psychological needs.

Needs	Physical or psychological conditions in human that act as stimuli for behaviour until satisfactions for them have been provided or achieved.
Network	A quantitative planning technique using activities and events to chart the flow of a project form start to finish and to calculate the shortest possible completion time for the project.
Objective	A goal to target than an individual or an organisation intends to achieve through planning and plans.
Objective performance appraisal	Appraisal system in which the criteria for performance and the rating scale are defined.
Operating plan	A plan that focuses on the implementation or ongoing part of a manager's planning responsibilities.
Organisation	A group of two or more people that exist and operates to achieve clearly stated, common objectives.
Organisation	The result of organising process; it consists of a whole make up of unified parts (a system), acting in harmony to execute tasks to achieve goals, in an effective an efficient manner.
Organisation chart	A visual representation of the way in which an entire organisation and each of its parts fit together.
Organising	The management activity that determines the work activities to be done, classifies and groups that work, assigns the activities and delegates authority to do the work, and designs a hierarchy of decision-making relationship.

Orientation Bringing a person into the specific working environment with emphasis on socialisation, the specific work, and the work environment.

Path-goal theory A leadership theory concerned with the ways in which a leader can influence a subordinate's motivation, goals, and attempts at goal achievement.

Payback analysis Evaluation of investment alternatives by comparing the length of time necessary to pay back their initial costs.

Performance appraisal A formal, structured system designed to measure an employee's actual performance against designated performance standards.

Planning Setting objectives and determining the means (courses of action) to reach those objectives.

Policy broad guidelines to aid managers at every level in making decisions about recruiting situations or functions.

Power A person's ability to influence results. It comes from expertise, charisma, or ability to reward or coerce, or from formal position.

Prevention control Monitoring devices or systems designed to establish conditions that will make it difficult or impossible for deviations from standards to occur.

Problem The difference between a desirable situation and what actually happens – the "what is" compared with "what should be."

Procedure	Plans that answer how to do something.
Programme	A single-use plan for solving a problem or accomplishing a group of related activities needed to reach a goal.
Programmed decision	Resolution by routine decision-making steps or procedures of a recurring challenge or problem.
Project	The overseeing of a project manager who must plan, organise, staff, direct, and control those tasks needed reach the desired outcome.
Promotion	Movement by a person into a position of higher pay and greater responsibilities.
Quality circle	A general planning technique involving workers and their supervisors in determining ways to improve methods, reduce waste and costs, and improve quality.
Queuing (waiting line) models	An operations research technique used to assist managers in deciding what length of waiting line or queue 'would be preferable.
Receiver	The person or persons intended as the audience for a message.
Recruitment	Finding people to meet the organisation's demands for special skill, aptitudes, knowledge, and experience.
Reinforcement theory	A motivation theory stating that the behaviour choices of a person are influenced by the supervisor's reactions to them and the rewards or penalties experienced in a similar situation.

Responsibility The obligation to carry one's assigned duties to the vest of 'one's ability.

Role Behaviours of managers is required to enact as he or she functions in the organisational environment. The role is influenced by the job description and the expectations of superiors, subordinates, and peers.

Rule Plans that dictate human behaviour or conduct at work.

Satisfice Make the best possible decision you can with the time and information you have available.

Selection Evaluating applicants and choosing the person who most closely meets job demands.

Sender The person or persons initiating a message.

Separation A temporary or permanent way or losing employees.

Simulation A model of a real or an actual or process that behaves like the real activity or process.

Span of control The principle of organisation that is concerned with the number of subordinates each manager should have to direct.

Staff authority Authority to serve in an advisory capacity; authority to advise.

Staff departments These assist all departments in meeting the objectives of the organisation through advice or technical assistance.

Staffing The management activity that attempts to attract good people to an organisation and to hold on to them.

Standard — A quantitative or qualitative measuring device designed to help monitor the performances of people, capital goods, or processes.

Standing plan — A predetermined course of action developed for repetitive situation

Strategic plan — A decision about long-range goals and the course of action to achieve those goals. Strategic plans influence the construction of tactical plans.

Strategic planning — Planning that focuses on organisational direction, involving all levels of management.

Subjective performance appraisal — Appraisal system in which the criteria for performance and the rating scale are not specifically defined.

System — A group of interrelated parts, operating as a whole, to achieve started goals or to function according to plan or design.

Tactical plan — A decision about short-term goals and the courses of action that will enable an organisation to achieve those goals. Tactical plans help achieve strategic goals.

Technical skill — The ability to use the processes, practices, techniques, and tools of the specialty area a manager supervises.

Therapeutic control — A monitoring device or system designed to sense what deviations form standards are taking place and why and then to take a corrective action.

Training Imparts skill, knowledge, and attitudes needed by individuals or groups to improve their abilities to perform in their present jobs.

Transfer A lateral move from one position to another having similar pay and a similar responsibility level.

Unity of command The organising principle that states that each person in an organisation should take orders from and report to only one person.

Unity of direction The organising principle that states that each group of activities having the same objective should have one head.

Variable costs Costs connected to the manufacture or sale of a product.

References

Boone, Louis E, and Kurtz, David, L., Principles of Management, 2nd Edition, USA Random House, Inc. 1984.

Brech, E.F.L., "Principles & Practices of Management", London: Longmans Green & Co., 1994, p. 6. UK.

Chabra, T.N., "Principles & Practice of Management", Dhanpat "Rai & Co., Fifth Edition, 1997, pp. 6-7.

Chandan J.S., Management Theory and Practice. New Delhi: Vikas Publishing House, VT. LTD. 2001, India.

Duncan, W.J., "Essential of Management", Illinois, Dryden Press Hisndale, USA, Jan, 1975, p. 4.

Durbin, Andrew J. Williams, J Clifton and Sisk, Henry L. Management and Organisation, Cincinnati: South-Western Publishing, 1985, USA.

Franklin, Terry, Principle of Management, 8th Edition Delhi: Vikas Publishing Company, 2001, India.

Gray, Jerry L. and Starke, Frederick A. Organisational Behaviour: Concepts and Applications, 3rd edition, Charles E. Merrill Publishing Co. 1984,USA.

Griffin, Ricky W., Management Theory and Practice; New York: McGraw-Hill Book Company, 1973, USA.

Harold Koontz and Cyril O'Donnell, "Principles of Management", 5th Edition, New: York, McGraw Hill, 1972, p. 1.

Ivancevich, John M. et.al Managing for Performance: An Introduction to the Process of Management; Texas: Business Publications, Inco., 1983, USA.

Ivancevich, Donnelly and Gibson, Management: Principles and Functions; 4th Edition, Boston, 1989, USA.

Kinard, Jerry, Management, D. C. Health and Company, 1988, USA.

Koontz, Harold, O Donnel, Gyrill, and Meinz Weihrch; Management; 9th Edition. New York: McGraw-Hill Book Company, 1988. USA.

Koontz, H. & Weibrich, H., "Essentials of Management", 5th Edition, McGraw Hill Publishing Company, U.S.A., 1990, p. 4.

Lundy, J.L. & Pradesh, P.C., "Organisation & Management", New Delhi: Porward Book Deptt., 1992, p. 8. Ibid, p. 8.

Luthans, Fred, Organisational Behavior, 3rd Edition, McGraw-Hill Book Company, 1981, USA.

Mathew, M.J., Business Management, Mc-Graw Hill Publishing Company 2000'.

Mitchell, Terence R., People in Organisations: An Introduction to Organisational Behavior, Second Edition, McGraw-Hill Book Company, 1982, USA.

Mittal A.K. & Agarwal S.B., "Principles of Management", 2nd Edition, Sanjeeva Prakash, Meerut Cantt, 1998, pp. 22-25.

Monaspa, Arun and Saiyadain Mirza, Personnel Management, 2nd Edition, New Delhi: Tata McGraw-Hill Company Limited, 1996, India.

Monks, Joseph G., Operations Management Theory and Practices, Second Edition, McGraw-Hill Book Company, 1982, USA.

Nakkiran S., Principles of Management, Coimbatore: Rainbow Publishing, 2001, India.

Narayana, P.S, Principle and Practice of Management, Delhi: Vikas Publishing Company 1987.

Pradesh, P.V., "Organisation & Management", Nirali Prakashan, Pune, 1992, pp. 13-15.

Plunkett, Warren R., and Attner, Raymond F., Introduction to Management; USA Kent Publishing Co. Boston, 1989.

Presthus, R, "The Organisation of Society, New York: Alfred A. Knopf, RNC. 1962.

Ramasamy, T, Principles of Management, Delhi: Himalaya Publishing House, 2001.

Robbins, S.P., "Management", 11th Edition, New Jersey: Prentice Hall, Englewood Cliffs, 1988, pp. 6-7. USA.

Robbins, Stephan p., Organisation Theory, Structure, Design and Applications. New Delhi: Prentice-Hall of India Private Limited, 1990, India.

Schwartz, David, Introduction to Management: Principles, Practices, and Processes, New York: Harcourt Brace Jovanovich, Inc., 1980, USA.

Sisk, Henry; Management and Organisation, 3rd Edition, Chicago: South Western Pub. Co. 1982, USA.

Stonner James A.F., Freeman R. Edwarad, and Gillbert Daniel R, Jr. Management, 6th Edition New Delhi: Prentice Hall, 1988, India.

Stoner, J.A. and Freeman, R.E. & Gilbert, D.R., "Management", 6th Edition, New Delhi: Prentice Hall of India Pvt. Ltd., 1996, p. 7.

Stonner James A.F., and Freeman R. Edward, Management, 5th Edition, New Jersey: Prentice-Hall, Eaglewood Cliffs, 1992, USA.

Varina, M.M. and Agarwal R.K. "Principles of Management", New Delhi: Forward Book Depot 1994, pp. 9-12

Yalokwu, P.O., Management Concepts and Techniques, Lagos: Peak Publishers, A Division of Consult LTD. 1999, Nigeria.

Index

E